THE
RISEN
REDEEMER

by

Timothy J. E. Cross

AMBASSADOR

BELFAST, NORTHERN IRELAND
GREENVILLE, SOUTH CAROLINA

The Risen Redeemer
© 2002 Timothy Cross

ISBN 1   84030 118 X

Ambassador Publications
a division of
Ambassador Productions Ltd.
Providence House
Ardenlee Street,
Belfast,
BT6 8QJ
Northern Ireland
www.ambassador-productions.com

Emerald House
427 Wade Hampton Blvd.
Greenville
SC 29609, USA
www.emeraldhouse.com

CONTENTS

	Page
Preface:	5
Chapter One: Matthew's Account of the First Easter Sunday	7
Chapter Two: Mark's Account of the First Easter Sunday	19
Chapter Three: Luke's Account of the First Easter Sunday	30
Chapter Four: A Heart Warming Encounter on the Emmaus Road	44
Chapter Five: John's Account of the First Easter Sunday Part I : The Empty Tomb	55
Chapter Six: John's Account of the First Easter Sunday Part II : The Risen Christ Appears to Mary Magdalene	64
Chapter Seven: Behind Closed Doors	73
Chapter Eight: The Saviour on the Shore	85
Epilogue	96

DEDICATION

I dedicate this book to Miss Ithwen John - an esteemed
senior sister in Christ, with whom it is my joy and
privilege to share Christian fellowship.

PREFACE

No event in history can compare with the resurrection of the Lord Jesus Christ from the dead. It was a momentous Event as it was an incomparable Event. It was an Event which transformed the world, and it was an Event which has transformed and still transforms countless individual lives.

In considering the resurrection, we are considering one of the Fundamental fundamentals of the Christian Faith. At the very centre of Biblical Christianity there is a vacated tomb.

Christ's resurrection has been described aptly as 'The most attested Fact in history.' Incredibly though, almost every Easter, some publicity seeking, unbelieving, infidel 'Christian' clergyman seeks to cast doubt on this incontestible fact and truth. Woe to such when they have to stand before the Almighty and give an account of their ministry! May this work be instrumental in dispelling any seeds of doubt which such evil men may have sown in the minds of the Lord's precious people.

In the following pages we will look at the Biblical evidence for the resurrection and the glorious and gracious implications of it for the Christian believer. My prayer is that as you read, you will become better grounded in the truth, and be drawn that much more closer to the Saviour Who certainly died and rose again for our eternal salvation.

I now cast this labour of love on the Tri-une God, with the prayer that His seal of approval will rest upon it. May He be pleased to use the pages which follow to bring blessing and edification to precious souls, and praise and glory to His ever blessed Name.

Sincere thanks to Mr Mostyn Davies of Wenvoe, Cardiff, for taking time from a busy schedule to help with the proofs.

Now may the God of peace Who brought again from the dead our Lord Jesus, the great shepherd of the sheep, by the blood of the eternal covenant, equip you with everything good that you may do His will, working in you that which is pleasing in His sight, through Jesus Christ; to Whom be glory for ever and ever. Amen (Hebrews 13:20).

Timothy J. E. Cross
Barry
South Wales

OTHER BOOKS BY THE SAME AUTHOR

MY FATHER'S HOUSE
Glimpses of the Glory

SCENT FROM HEAVEN
The Lovely Fragrance of Jesus

WALKING WITH JESUS
Milestones in the Life of Christ

COMFORT FROM THE BIBLE
Help for those who Hurt

A STRING OF PEARLS
Treasures from the Bible

A POSTCARD FROM PAUL
(Paul's letter to Philemon)

THE LORD'S MY SHEPHERD,
I'LL NOT WANT . . . (Psalm 23)

WATER FROM THE WELL
Refreshment fromthe Bible

Available from:

Ambassador Productions Ltd
Providence House
Ardenlee Street
BELFAST
BT6 8QJ

Chapter One

Matthew's Account of the First Easter Sunday

Now after the Sabbath, toward the dawn of the first day of the week, Mary Magdalene and the other Mary went to see the sepulchre. And behold, there was a great earthquake; for an angel of the Lord descended from heaven and came and rolled back the stone, and sat upon it. His appearance was like lightning, and his raiment white as snow. And for fear of him the guards trembled and became like dead men. But the angel said to the women, 'Do not be afraid; for I know that you seek Jesus Who was crucified. He is not here; for He has risen, as He said. Come, see the place where He lay. Then go quickly and tell His disciples that He has risen from the dead, and behold, He is going before you to Galilee; there you will see Him. Lo, I have told you.'

So they departed quickly from the tomb with fear and great joy, and ran to tell His disciples. And behold, Jesus met them and said, 'Hail!' And they came up and took hold of His feet and worshipped Him. Then Jesus said to them, 'Do not be afraid; go and tell my brethren to go to Galilee, and there they will see Me' (Matthew 28:1-10).

Introduction

When the Lord Jesus died on Calvary's cross, Pontius Pilate made a placard. This placard was nailed to the cross above the Lord Jesus's head. According to Matthew, the placard said:- *'This is Jesus the King of the Jews'* (Matthew 27:37). There are only eight words here, in English - yet these eight words actually summarise the whole twenty eight chapters of Matthew's Gospel.

Matthew's purpose in writing his Gospel is to introduce us to the King - King Jesus. Matthew, being the first book of the New Testament, is the ideal bridge between the two testaments, because Matthew shows without a doubt that Jesus is the fulfilment of all the Old Testament hopes, longings, prophecies and aspirations.

Many times in the Old Testament, God promised that, one day, He would send the Messiah - the Messiah Who would bring in the blessed Kingdom of Heaven. Matthew shows clearly that in Jesus, God's promises were fulfilled. He shows in his Gospel that Jesus is the longed for Messiah and King - 'Great David's Greater Son.'

> Hail to the Lord's Anointed
> Great David's greater Son!
> Hail, in the time appointed
> His reign on earth begun!
> He comes to break oppression
> To set the captive free
> To take away transgression
> And rule in equity.

Kings are characterised by authority, and Christ's kingly authority is evident from every page of Matthew's Gospel. But never more so was this than now, in Christ's resurrection from the dead. Never was Christ's kingly authority demonstrated more clearly than when He conquered the grave. Matthew's Gospel is a Gospel of a King Who died and came back to life. King Jesus was a totally victorious King, as we shall now see, as we consider Matthew's account of Christ's victorious rising from the dead on the first Easter morning.

An Earth Shattering Event

A certain Hollywood film director once allegedly said words to the effect that 'The secret of a good film is to begin with an earthquake, and then work up to a climax.' Whether this film director was acquainted with Matthew's Gospel is uncertain, but Matthew's account of Christ's resurrection certainly does begin with an earthquake, and then, if anything, the proceedings get even more climactic!

The resurrection of the Lord Jesus Christ certainly was an earth shattering event, literally and metaphorically. Matthew's account of the resurrection records at the outset *And behold, there was a great earthquake; for an angel of the Lord descended from heaven and came and rolled back the stone, and sat upon it* (v.2).

Earthquakes frighten us because they are wild and destructive. There is nothing like an earthquake to make us aware of our human puniness and impotence. Earthquakes fill us with fear because they are so beyond our control. Interestingly though, the Bible shows that key events on God's calendar are often accompanied by earthquakes. They all demonstrate God's omnipotent power, and remind us that He is in total control:-

When the Lord gave the Law on Mount Sinai, the Bible tells us that *His voice then shook the earth* (Hebrews 12:26). When Christ died at Calvary, Matthew recorded in the previous chapter that *the earth shook and the rocks were split* (Matthew 27:51). When Christ comes again in power and great glory there will also be an earthquake, for God has promised *Yet once more I will shake not only the earth but also the heaven* (Hebrews 12:26). All this being so, it comes as less of a surprise to see that on the first Easter Day there *was a great earthquake.* For Christ's resurrection from the dead is a key Event in Biblical history, central and integral to God's plan of bringing salvation to His people and glory to His name.

Matthew was a former tax collector. His job depended on his accountability and careful, accurate record keeping. With him as our dependable guide then, let us go back, in our mind's eye to the Garden Tomb, on the morning of the first Easter Sunday - the Day of Resurrection. First of all, we note:-

1. The Messenger

. . . Mary Magdalene and the other Mary went to see the sepulchre. And behold, there was a great earthquake; for an <u>angel of the Lord</u> descended from heaven and came and rolled back the stone and sat upon it. His appearance was like lightning, and his raiment white as snow (vv.1-3).

The Greek word for 'angel' - angelos - means 'messenger'. All four Gospel accounts tell us that angels were present when Christ rose from the dead - just as angels were also present at key stages in the life and ministry of the Lord Jesus:-

It was an angel who announced the Good News of the Saviour's birth. It was an angel who previously informed Mary concerning the virgin womb into which the eternal Christ entered - just as here it is an angel who informs us of the virgin tomb out of which Christ exited. It was an angel who strengthened Christ as He contemplated the horror of Calvary in Gethsemane's garden. Angels were there also when Christ ascended back to heaven, forty days after this Easter Day. 1 Thessalonians 4:16 informs us that it is the archangel's call which will summon the glorious Second Coming of Christ - a Coming which will bring a culmination and climax to all history. How fitting therefore that here, on the epochal morning of Christ's resurrection, Matthew informs us of the presence of an angel - *the angel of the Lord.*

Christ had risen. His body was no longer embalmed in the tomb. So the angel of the Lord rolled away the stone - only super human strength would suffice.

Three days before this time, the Romans, under Pontius Pilate, had crucified Christ. Christ's crucifixion had caused such an uproar, and the Jewish establishment was so hostile to Jesus, that, having crucified Him, it was felt necessary to have a police guard over His grave. Matthew 27:62 ff. relates how *the chief priests and the Pharisees gathered before Pilate and said, 'Sir, we remember how that impostor said, while He was still alive, 'After three days I will rise again.' Therefore order the sepulchre to be made secure until the third day, lest His disciples go and steal Him away, and tell the people 'He has risen from the dead,' and the last fraud will be worse than the first.' Pilate said to them, 'You have a guard of soldiers; go, make it as secure as you can.' So they went and made the sepulchre secure by sealing the stone and setting a guard.*

To us, the stone, seal and sentry seem most intimidating. But actually, how very weak they really were, for the angel broke the seal, rolled away the stone and sat upon it. The guards, so tough in the eyes of the world, *trembled and became like dead men* (v.4). Christ had won a complete and absolute victory over the grave! *The last enemy to be destroyed is death* (1 Corinthians 15:26), and the rolled stone, broken seal and empty tomb are graphic evidence of Christ's triumphant conquest of the last enemy. The angel rolled away the stone, not to let Christ out - for He was already risen - but to let the women and other witnesses in to see the evidence with their own eyes.

> Vain the stone, the watch, the seal
> Christ hath burst the gates of hell
> Death in vain forbids Him rise
> Christ has opened Paradise!

The angelic messenger was sent from heaven to do heaven's bidding. He *came and rolled back the stone and sat upon it.* As yet, the angel had not spoken a word, but his very posture of sitting upon that massive boulder, speaks volumes concerning the victory which Christ had won over death:-

> Vainly they watch His bed - Jesus my Saviour
> Vainly they seal the dead - Jesus my Lord
>
> Death cannot keep his pray - Jesus my Saviour
> He tore the bars away - Jesus my Lord
>
> Up from the grave He arose
> With a mighty triumph o'er His foes
> He arose a Victor from the dark domain

And He lives for ever with His saints to reign
He arose! He arose!
Hallelujah! Christ arose!

Christ, therefore, was no longer in the prison of the tomb. Imagine, for a moment, being in a prison cell. You have been sentenced there for many years, but then the day comes . . . and the door of your cell is opened. The guard says "You have served your sentence now. You have paid the price for your crime. Now you may go free."

On the Cross, Christ paid the price for our sins. He served our death sentence there in full. Having paid the price for our sins, He went free. Our sins were imputed to Him. He made full satisfaction for them, and having done so, He was acquitted by God. The Good News is that His acquittal is our acquittal, if we are trusting in Him for our salvation. Romans 4:25 states that *Jesus our Lord . . . was put to death for our trespasses and raised for our justification.*

It is through the death and resurrection of Jesus that the believer's sins are forgiven and we, the guilty ones, are declared 'Not guilty' by God. The guiltless One took our guilt, that we might be freed. God the Father was completely satisfied with the atoning death of Christ in our place. To seal His approval, He raised His Son from the grave. Christ arose! *For we know that Christ being raised from the dead will never die again; death no longer has dominion over Him* (Romans 6:9).

The angel though had an Easter message to give. Let us look at this next:-

2. The Message

The angel's message was clear and unmistakable: *'He is not here; for He has risen, as He said. Come, see the place where He lay'* (v.6).

HE HAS RISEN! That is the message of Easter. HE HAS RISEN! That is the message of the Christian Faith, for the Christian Faith is founded on the unshakable and immovable rock of Christ's resurrection. The earliest ever distillation of the basic fundamentals of the Christian Faith included the line: *He was raised on the third day in accordance with the Scriptures* (1 Corinthians 15:4). This early creed though was only putting into credal form the events of this first Easter morning: *He is not here; for He has risen, as He said. Come see the place where He lay.*

> Come, ye saints, look here and wonder
> See the place where Jesus lay
> He has burst His bands asunder
> He has borne our sins away
> Joyful tidings, joyful tidings
> Yes, the Lord is risen today.

i. The resurrection confirms the worth of Christ

The Christian Faith is a resurrection Faith. The Christian Faith actually stands or falls on the truth of Christ's resurrection, for it is this which is the ultimate and final proof of the Deity of Christ, that is, that Jesus Christ is none less than 'the only begotten Son of God, begotten of His Father before all worlds, God of God, Light of Light, very God of very God, Begotten not made, being of one substance with the Father.' The reality of Christ's resurrection confirms the reality of Christ's Person - that He really is the Person He claimed to be and the Person that the Bible consistently and persistently declares that He is: *'I am the resurrection and the life'* (John 11:25).*Who was . . . designated Son of God in power according to the Spirit of holiness by His resurrection from the dead, Jesus Christ our Lord* (Romans 1:4).

ii. The resurrection confirms the words of Christ

Notice carefully the exact words which the angel said on that first Easter morning. *'He is not here; for He has risen, as He said.'* It is easy to gloss over those three words *as He said*. But they remind us that Christ had indeed prophesied His Own resurrection from the grave. The fact that Christ's prophecies in this realm did not seem to have registered with His disciples, does not detract from the fact that He made such prophecies in the first place. Let us recap on some of the words which Christ spoke, recorded by Matthew, which clearly foretold this first Easter day:-

From that time, Jesus began to show His disciples that He must go to Jerusalem and suffer many things from the elders and chief priests and scribes, and be killed, <u>and on the third day be raised</u> (Matthew 16:21).

'Tell no one the vision, until the Son of Man is <u>risen from the dead</u> (Matthew 17:9)

'The Son of Man is to be delivered into the hands of men, and they will kill Him; and <u>He will be raised on the third day</u> (Matthew 17:23)

'Behold, we are going up to Jerusalem; and the Son of Man will be delivered to the chief priests and scribes, and they will condemn Him to death, and they will deliver Him to the Gentiles to be mocked and scourged and crucified, and <u>He will be raised on the third day</u> (Matthew 20:18,19).

So we can see that Christ's resurrection was all too clearly foretold by Him; it was just AS HE SAID!

From all of this we can see that we have very good reason to depend on the words of the Lord Jesus Christ. All He spoke was true. The resurrection proves that He is the Messiah - our prophet, priest and king. Consider His role as a prophet. We have seen that He predicted His Own resurrection. Prophets claiming to know the future have always been around. This being so, the Bible, in Deuteronomy 18:22 gives us the test to decide whether a prophet is a true one or a false one, that is, whether divinely appointed or self-appointed. Deuteronomy 18:22 reads: *When a prophet speaks in the name of the LORD, if the word does not come to pass or come true, that is a word which the LORD has not spoken.* The words which the Lord Jesus spoke though definitely did come to pass. They all came true. His prophecies were fulfilled, and He was raised on the third day, just AS HE SAID. We have therefore just cause to depend on Christ and His word. In John 11:25,26 Christ made the stupendous claim: *I am the resurrection and the life; he who believes in Me, though he die, yet shall he live, and whoever lives and believes in Me shall never die.* Here as elsewhere, Jesus spoke the truth. His resurrection shows that we may believe His words and stake our eternal well-being on them.

The message of the first Easter morning was a message of comfort - *Do not be afraid,* and it was a message of conquest: *He is not here; for He has risen as He said.* The message though was addressed to some unusual people - normal people, for sure, but unusual in the sense that if this was fiction, surely these people would not have been written into the script . . .

3. The Marys

. . . *toward the dawn of the first day of the week, Mary Magdalene and the other Mary went to see the sepulchre* (v.1).

Here we have two Marys. They not only shared the same name, but they also shared the same devotion to the Saviour. It is an astonishing fact that the first ever witnesses to the resurrection of Christ were women - and women of a not very high rank in society at large. Matthew's record says that it was these two Marys who were the first to witness both the empty tomb and the physical presence of the risen Lord. The Law of Moses states that only on *the evidence of two witnesses, or of three witnesses, shall a charge be sustained . . . A single witness shall not prevail* (Deuteronomy 19:15). Here then are the two witnesses which substantiate the case.

In the ancient world, prejudice was such that women were not allowed to give evidence in court. The fact that the first witnesses to the resurrection are shown to be women, suggests that the Gospel records cannot be the work of a forger. These female witnesses are one of the many proofs of the veracity and total integrity of the resurrection accounts. If this had all been made up, surely Christ would have appeared first of all to, say, Peter, or the High Priest, or the Sanhedrin, or even to the

Emperor. But to two women? It just goes to show that here we are dealing with reality not mythology, fact and not fiction, God's inspired truth rather than man's invented tales.

The first witnesses to the resurrection of Christ then were women. In the world of the Bible, 'women's liberation' was an unknown concept. As an aside, we may say that no one has done more for women's liberation than the Lord Jesus Christ. Whilst the Bible teaches a distinction in role between the two genders, the Bible is equally clear that in Christ, men and women are equal in status. Both are made in the image of God and both may enjoy the blessings of His eternal salvation. *There is neither Jew nor Greek, there is neither male nor female; for you are all one in Christ Jesus* (Galatians 3:28).

The women's witness

Notice briefly the command which was given to the two Marys. The command actually encapsulates an eternal principle. Verse 6: *Come, see the place where He lay. Then go quickly and tell His disciples that He has risen from the dead.*

i. Come and see. ii. Go and tell. Christian testimony is based and can only be based on first hand experience. We cannot share what we do not have. How can we speak about something which we do not know? Once we experience the risen life of Christ in our souls however, we will want to share this joy with others. Come and see. Go and tell. Surely this is the essence of personal evangelism. Informal evangelism -'gossiping the Gospel' - is the overflow of a heart full of the joy of the Lord. A mind convinced of God's truth, a heart inflamed with God's love and a soul indwelt by God's Spirit . . . Telling others about Jesus has perhaps been made out to be more difficult than it really is. The early disciples had no formal schooling in evangelism, but how they shared the Gospel with all and sundry. Good News is for sharing. *We cannot but speak of what we have seen and heard* (Acts 4:21). It was harder for them to contain their joy than it was to share it!

Returning to Matthew's narrative, we see that the women

were obedient to the angelic command, for *they departed quickly from the tomb with fear and great joy, and ran to tell the disciples* (v.8). And on this path of obedience, Who should they encounter but the Risen Master Himself.

4. The Master

And behold, Jesus met them and said 'Hail!' And they came up and took hold of His feet and worshipped Him (v.9).

The evidence for Christ's resurrection may be put into two broad categories. 1. There is the fact of the empty tomb. 2. There is the fact of the risen, physical presence of Christ Himself. We are moving now into this second category.*Behold, Jesus met them . . . And they came up and took hold of His feet and worshipped Him.* Jesus met them! 'On the third day He arose from the dead, with the same body in which He suffered' (*Westminster Confession of Faith*). *Behold, Jesus met them!*

Lo! Jesus meets us, risen from the tomb
Lovingly He greets us, scatters fear and gloom
Let the church with gladness, hymns of triumph sing
For her Lord now liveth, death has lost its sting.

Matthew records here how that Jesus both meets the women and greets the women. *'Hail!'* This greeting is the word 'Chairete' in the Greek original. It is a word which can be translated 'Rejoice!' Some however translate it as 'Grace to you. Health to you.' Perhaps the word encompasses both meanings. Chairete! It is the message of joy and gladness of the first Easter morning - a joy and gladness which is still imparted by the risen Saviour, even today. *Blessed be the God and Father of our Lord Jesus Christ! By His great mercy we have been born anew to a living hope through the resurrection of Jesus Christ from the dead* (1 Peter 1:3).

Finally, note the reference here to both the humanity and the deity of the risen Saviour when *they took hold of His feet and worshipped Him*.

i. His Humanity

. . . they took hold of His feet. This shows that Christ's resurrection was a physical one and not a phantasmal one. Those who speak of illusions or some vague 'Christ living on in the memory' have no explanation for the women's taking hold of Christ's feet here - just as they cannot explain the risen Christ's eating a piece of broiled fish in Luke 24:42,43. In Christ though we know that our God is human too. He shared our human lot, sin apart⋅ He knows what it is to live in these bodies of clay. *We have not a high priest Who is unable to sympathise with our weaknesses* (Hebrews 4:15). Matthew's account of the resurrection however not only shows the humanity of the risen Saviour, but also:-

ii. His Deity

. . . they . . .worshipped Him. A basic Biblical axiom is that God alone is to be worshipped. *You shall worship the Lord your God and Him only shall you serve* (Matthew 4:10). Worshipping anyone or anything other than God is committing the sin of idolatry. Here however Jesus was worshipped by the women and He did not rebuke them for idolatry. He accepted their worship. It goes to show that Jesus Christ is God - the Son of God and God the Son - co-equal and co-eternal with the Father and the Holy Spirit, ever to be worshipped and adored. His triumph over the tomb here, as described by Matthew, is actually the ultimate proof of His Deity and the ultimate proof that He alone has power to save. The women thus did what the individual believer also does in spirit every day. Bowing, and taking hold of His feet *they worshipped Him.* None compares with this risen Saviour. *God has highly exalted Him and bestowed on Him the name which is above every name, that at the name of Jesus every knee should bow, in heaven and on earth and under the earth, and every tongue confess that Jesus Christ is Lord to the glory of God the Father* (Philippians 2:9,10).

Chapter Two

Mark's Account of the
First Easter Sunday

And when the Sabbath was past, Mary Magdalene, and Mary the mother of James, and Salome, bought spices, so that they might go and anoint Him. And very early on the first day of the week they went to the tomb when the sun had risen. And they were saying to one another, 'Who will roll away the stone for us from the door of the tomb?' And looking up, they saw that the stone was rolled back - it was very large. And entering the tomb, they saw a young man sitting on the right side, dressed in a white robe; and they were amazed. And he said to them, 'Do not be amazed; you seek Jesus of Nazareth, Who was crucified. He has risen, He is not here; see the place where they laid Him. But go, tell His disciples and Peter that He is going before you to Galilee; there you will see Him, as He told you.' And they went out and fled from the tomb; for trembling and astonishment had come upon them; and they said nothing to any one, for they were afraid (Mark 16:1-8).

Introduction

Common scholarly consent considers Mark's Gospel to be the earliest of the four Gospel accounts of the life and ministry of Jesus. We have therefore just read the earliest ever narration of the events of the morning of the first Easter Sunday.

Mark's Gospel was written in about 65 AD to a community in Rome. An early tradition states that Mark gained the information for his fast-moving Gospel from none less than the

Apostle Peter. Peter was one of the inner three of the twelve disciples and Mark himself was Peter's 'Personal Assistant'. Unbeknown to him, his racy written account of Peter's reminiscences, under the inspiration of the Holy Spirit, in due time, was to make him one of the best selling authors ever.

Mark's particular 'slant' on the Lord Jesus is his portrayal of Him as the Servant of the Lord. In a verse which gives the key to all of Mark's sixteen chapters - Mark 10:45 - we read *The Son of Man came not to be served but to serve and to give His life as a ransom for many.* It is the sacrifice of the Servant, as described in Mark 15, which saves. It sets the believer free. It ransoms us from the penalty and power of sin. The resurrection of the Servant in chapter 16 though is the complement of this sacrifice. It is the other side of the 'salvation coin,' for God's very Own raising of the servant Christ from the dead is the clear evidence of His divine approval of the Servant's sacrifice. The resurrection gives us cause to be assured and re-assured that our sins really have been paid for in full by Christ on the Cross. The resurrection of Christ is the divine 'receipt' of Christ's sacrificial payment - God's 'received with thanks', if you like. Mark's evidence for Christ's resurrection shows that if we are trusting in the sacrifice of Christ, salvation has been bought for us by Him, and there is nothing else for us to pay, now or eternally.

Before we look in a little more detail at some of the activities told of by Mark in his account of the first Easter morning, let us have a brief reminder of the background to this epochal Easter event:-

The Background

On the first 'Good Friday' - day one - the Lord Jesus was crucified. Crucifixion was one of the most savage forms of capital punishment ever invented. Although the Lord Jesus was cruelly killed, He was very lovingly buried. Joseph of Arimathea and Nicodemus the Pharisee carefully embalmed His sacred body with spices and bandages. They then *laid Him in a tomb which had been hewn out of the rock; and rolled a stone against the door of the tomb* (Mark 15:46). In this tomb, the Lord's body rested for the whole of the Jewish Sabbath - day two - our Saturday. Interestingly, Genesis 2:2 tells us that at the work of Creation *On the seventh day God finished His work which He had done, and He rested on the seventh day from all His work which He had done.* As God the Father rested from His completed work of Creation on the seventh day, it was therefore most fitting for God the Son to similarly rest from His completed work of redemption on the seventh day too. For the whole of the seventh day, Jesus's body lay in the cool of a rock tomb. Mark notes that *Mary Magdalene and Mary the mother of Joses saw where He was laid* (Mark 15:47). This now takes us to day three, the first day of the week, our Sunday. It is a day for ever sanctified by the events we are about to consider. An early Christian creed tells us why, when it says of Christ: *He was buried . . . and that He was raised on the third day in accordance with the Scriptures* (1 Corinthians 15:3,4).

Having set the scene then, we can now look at Mark's account of the first Easter a little more closely. We note first of all that it involved:-

1. The Anointing

And when the Sabbath was past, Mary Magdalene, and Mary the mother of James, and Salome, bought spices, so that they might go and anoint Him (v.1).

Mark is silent as to these women's exact motives for wanting to go and anoint the body of the Lord Jesus. We could speculate and suggest that perhaps they thought that Joseph and Nicodemus's work was not as thorough as it might have been. Joseph and Nicodemus worked fearfully, and would have had to work rather hurriedly to complete the task before the Sabbath . . . Whatever the women's reasons, their devotion to the Saviour stands out. In their own minds, Jesus was dead. This now was to be their last act of love and devotion to Him. Love has its own reasons. Love is lavish. Love is somewhat blind to difficulties in the way. Love goes the second mile. So early on that Sunday morning, Mary, Mary and Salome *bought spices, so that they might go and anoint Him.*

The Anointed One

The word 'Christ' means 'Anointed One' The Greek word 'chrism' means 'oil', and the Greek word 'Christos' refers to one anointed with oil. The Hebrew for 'Christos' is 'Messiah'.

The Jews longed for the Messiah - God's Agent Who would come in His Own time and bring in the blessed kingdom of heaven. In Jesus, the Messiah came. Mark had earlier related Peter's admission to Jesus *You are the Christ* (Mark 8:29). 'Christ' is actually a title, rather than a name. The title speaks volumes about the work which Jesus came to do.

In Old Testament times, Israelite prophets, priests and kings were all considered to be lesser agents of God Himself, when they were truly called and ordained by Him. As such, these were all thought of as 'God's anointed.' Before they began their respective ministries, they were therefore anointed with oil. It symbolised their being set apart by God and divinely equipped by the Holy Spirit for the task that God would have them do:-

i. Prophets were anointed with oil. For instance, God commanded Elijah: *Elisha the Son of Shaphat . . . you shall anoint to be prophet in your place* (1 Kings 19:16).

ii. Priests were anointed with oil. Their task of sacrificing animals was central to the Old Testament economy, teaching that *without the shedding of blood there is no forgiveness of sins* (Hebrews 9:2). The Old Testament sacrificial priesthood was no light office. Those who were called to it therefore received a solemn ordination and anointing: *And you shall anoint Aaron and his sons, and consecrate them, that they may serve Me as priests . . .* (Exodus 30:30).

iii. Kings were anointed with oil. Saul was Israel's first king, and 1 Samuel 10:1 relates how *Samuel took a vial of oil and poured it on his head, and kissed him and said, "Has not the LORD anointed you to be prince over His people Israel? . . .* David was Israel's greatest earthly king, and a clear 'type' of Christ - great David's Greater Son. 1 Samuel 16:3 records how *Samuel took the horn of oil, and anointed him in the midst of his brothers; and the*

Spirit of the LORD came mightily upon David from that day forward.
    As *the* Anointed One, Christ fulfils the three-fold office of
prophet, priest and king in His One Person. The *Shorter Catechism* expresses it very clearly:-

> Christ executeth the office of a
> prophet in revealing to us, by His
> Word and Spirit, the will of God for
> our salvation.
> Christ executeth the office of a priest
> in His once offering up of Himself a
> sacrifice to satisfy divine justice, and
> reconcile us to God, and in making
> continual intercession for us.
> Christ executeth the office of a king,
> in subduing us to Himself, in ruling
> and defending us, and in restraining
> and conquering all His and our en-
> emies.

    So three women came to anoint the body of Jesus. Their
action was well meant, if misguided. We have seen though that
their action was not entirely inappropriate.

2. The Anguish

The Great Sadness

    We can only surmise the anguished emotions of the three
grief stricken women as they made their way to Jesus's burial
site. Mark sensitively omits a detailed description of their sorrow when *very early on the first day of the week they went to the
tomb when the sun had risen. And they were saying to one another,
'Who will roll away the stone for us from the door of the tomb?'* (vv.2,3).
    Mark's account of the resurrection has a sober ring of truth
about it throughout. Fiction would no doubt have described
these three women as running to the tomb to worship a living

Saviour. The fact was however, that in their own minds, they were going to pay their last respects to a dead Friend. Their embalming of Jesus was to be their final act of devotion to Him - a devotion which, incidentally, was to be greatly rewarded. The thought of Jesus's rising from the dead, at this stage, was a thought which just was not in their mental frame of reference. The Old Testament prophecies, along with Jesus's Own foretelling of His rising from the dead, evidently had not gripped their minds and hearts. They just did not expect the resurrection of the Lord Jesus. With the advantage of our hindsight, when the Church has celebrated Christ's resurrection for two thousand years or so, it is easy for us to overlook the fact that these women's expectations of ever seeing Jesus again were absolutely zero.

The Great Stone

Humanly, these women's desire and devotion was physically thwarted by one thing: a great stone. *'Who will roll away the stone for us from the door of the tomb?'* (v.3).

The women here are implying that the heavy manual work of shifting an enormous boulder necessitated the labour of some strong men. The women seem to be confessing that they just did not feel up to the task. Removing the huge stone from Jesus's tomb was not a job for women - but then it was also not a job for men either. The truth is that the stone which barred entry to Jesus's tomb was moved miraculously by God Himself. Matthew 28:2 tells how God had already sent an earthquake just a little before the women arrived. The result of this divine shaking was now evidenced plainly by these women. The barrier to the tomb had been removed and hence the women's difficulty had been removed. *And looking up, they saw that the stone was rolled back - it was very large* (v.4). David Brown at this point makes a very encouraging practical application when he asks:-'And are there no others who, when advancing to duty in the face of appalling difficulties, find their stone rolled away?' Our God is infinitely able!

3. The Angel

If the two Marys and Salome did not expect to encounter an open tomb on the first Easter morning, they certainly did not expect to encounter any angels either. Such a meeting is not exactly an every day occurrence. Mark's account, however, continues by relating how that on *entering the tomb, they saw a young man sitting on the right side, dressed in a white robe; and they were amazed* (v.5). Such a spontaneous amazement is very understandable. If we put all four Gospel accounts together, we see that there were actually two angels present - though Mark here chooses to focus solely on the spokesman of the two.

The evidence of all four Gospels shows that no human being was considered worthy of being present at the actual moment of Christ's resurrection. Sinless, angelic beings though were permitted by God to be there. These then related the Good News of Christ's resurrection to His followers. An early Christian hymn goes:- *Great indeed, we confess, is the mystery of our religion: God was manifested in the flesh, vindicated in the Spirit, seen by angels, preached among the nations, believed on in the world, taken up in glory* (1 Timothy 3:16). A contemporary hymn also takes this up, and celebrates how:-

The Spirit vindicated Christ our Lord
And angels sang with joy and sweet accord
The nations heard, a dark world flamed with light -
When Jesus rose in glory and in might.

We often overlook the ministry of angels in relation to the ministry of the Lord Jesus Christ. It was an angel who announced the Good News of Christ's birth - *to you is born this day, in the city of David, a Saviour Who is Christ the Lord* (Luke 2:10). And when Christ was born, the very skies were filled with angelic praise: *And suddenly there was with the angel a multitude of the heavenly host, praising God and saying, 'Glory to God in the highest, and on earth peace, good will among men'* (Luke 2:13,14). Christ's Second

Coming will also be accompanied by *the archangel's call, and the sound of the trumpet of God* (1 Thessalonians 4:16). Then there was that time in the garden of Gethsemene. There, as Christ prayerfully considered the impending agony of the cross of Calvary, and something of the horror of the sufferings He was about to undergo swept over His soul, an angel came to His aid. *And there appeared to Him an angel from heaven, strengthening Him* (Luke 22:43). Angelic appearances at Christ's resurrection are therefore in keeping with other crucial stages in His life and ministry.

The word 'angel' means 'messenger.' This particular angel was now about to fulfil his role and announce the greatest Message ever. Note carefully the angel's central announcement:-

4. The Announcement

And he said to them, 'Do not be amazed; you seek Jesus of Nazareth, Who was crucified. He has risen, He is not here; see the place where they laid Him (v.6). Mark's Gospel now reaches its culmination and climax. (*He*) *was crucified. He has risen . . . see the place where they laid Him.*

Come, ye saints, look here and wonder
See the place where Jesus lay
He has burst His bands asunder
He has borne our sins away
Joyful tidings!
Yes, the Lord is risen today

Jesus triumphs! O sing praises!
By His death He overcame
Thus the Lord His glory raises
Thus He fills His foes with shame
O sing praises!
Praises to the Victor's name.

It is striking that the angel mentions the death of Christ, as well as His resurrection in this central announcement. *(He) was crucified. He has risen.* Both the death and the resurrection of Christ are central and integral to the Christian Message. We cannot have one without the other. One gives meaning to the other. If Christ had not died, the penalty for our sin would not have been paid. If Christ had not been raised, His death was just an ordinary death, and not an atoning death. Central to the whole Christian Faith therefore is the death and the resurrection of the Lord Jesus Christ, with all its saving significance. The death and the resurrection of the Lord Jesus Christ constitutes the Gospel which the Church proclaims - and there is no other Gospel. *Jesus our Lord . . . was put to death for our trespasses and raised for our justification* (Romans 4:25). *I delivered to you as of first importance . . . that Christ died for our sins in accordance with the Scriptures, that He was buried, that He was raised on the third day in accordance with the Scriptures* (1 Corinthians 15:3,4).

The angel though had more to say. He had some marching orders for the women!

Angelic Orders

But go, tell His disciples and Peter, that He is going before you to Galilee; there you will see Him as He told you (v.7).

The disciples were also known as 'the apostles'. 'An apostle' means 'one who is sent.' Acts 1:22 states that the main qualification and role of an apostle was that of being a *witness of His resurrection*. How ironic then that these women were commanded to be apostles to the apostles. The women were actually sent to tell the disciples that Christ had conquered the grave. When we consider the much lower status that women had in the ancient world, we realise that all this is beyond the ingenuity of the most creative of human imaginations. No one would have invented this. It all happened just as Mark recorded.

tell His disciples and Peter. Peter, of course, was a disciple on an equal par with the others. Yet it is lovely that he is singled out. Having recently failed his Lord in denying Him three times, how glad he must have been to know that there was still room for him in Jesus's heart and God's future purposes. God's continuing grace and faithfulness must have been a great comfort to Peter. God's continuing grace is also a great comfort to us. We fail our Lord. We deny Him in so many ways . . . yet He does not cast us off or out. There is restorative grace with Him. Who knows just what purposes and plans He may yet have in store for us in the future, inspite of the failures we have been to date . . .

He is going before you to Galilee; there you will see Him. Matthew 28:16 ff. and John 21 show that this actually came to pass. The disciples were eventually reunited with the risen Lord in the familiar surroundings of Galilee, just as Jesus had previously told them that they would be. *as He told you.* In Mark 14:28 Jesus stated definitely *But after I am raised up, I will go before you to Galilee.* From this we see that God keeps His Word and that the Son of God also keeps His Word. In a world which so often reveals itself as untrustworthy, it is good to know that in Christ we have a God on Whom we can totally depend. *God is not man, that He should lie, or a son of man, that He should repent. Has He said, and will He not do it? Or has He spoken, and will He not fulfil it* (Numbers 23:19).

Finally, we note the women's reaction to all of this. It was one of amazement, astonishment and not a little fear:-

5. The Astonishment

And they went out and fled from the tomb; for trembling and astonishment had come upon them; and they said nothing to any one, for they were afraid (v.8).

We can safely say that we are not dealing with a story of human heroism here! Mark's account of Christ's resurrection reveals Christ's deity for sure - taking us back in full circle to his opening verse *The beginning of the Gospel of Jesus Christ, the Son of God* (Mark 1:1). Along with the truth of Christ's deity however, we have the equal truth of the humanity of Christ's followers. *they went out and fled . . . trembling and astonishment had come upon them . . . they were afraid.*

We would not have expected Mark to conclude his account of the first Easter morning - not to mention the whole of his Gospel - in this way. Again though, we see that Mark was just not at liberty to make things up, or to tidy things up for the reporting. Mark is only telling it all the way that it was - reporting the sane and sober truth. The women were so shocked that initially they were dumb struck. *they said nothing to any one* - neither to Christ's friends nor His enemies. Yet 'truth will out.' Eventually they overcame their initial shock and went to the disciples and told them the Good News - the same Good News which has been told and celebrated by the Church from that day to the present, and will continue to be told until the Risen Redeemer returns in glory.

Yes, the Redeemer rose
The Saviour left the dead
And oe'r our hellish foes
High raised His conquering head
In wild dismay
The guards around
Fell to the ground
And sunk away

All hail, triumphant Lord
Who sav'st us with Thy blood!
Wide be Thy Name adored
Thou risen, reigning God!
With Thee we rise
With Thee we reign
And empires gain
Beyond the skies.

Chapter Three

Luke's Account of the First Easter Sunday

But on the first day of the week, at early dawn, they went to the tomb, taking the spices which they had prepared. And they found the stone rolled away from the tomb, but when they went in they did not find the body. While they were perplexed about this, behold, two men stood by them in dazzling apparel; and as they were frightened and bowed their faces to the ground, the men said to them, 'Why do you seek the living among the dead? Remember how He told you, while He was still in Galilee, that the Son of Man must be delivered into the hands of sinful men, and be crucified, and on the third day rise.' And they remembered His words, and returning from the tomb they told all this to the eleven and to all the rest. Now it was Mary Magdalene and Joanna and Mary the mother of James and the other women with them who told this to the apostles; but these words seemed to them an idle tale, and they did not believe them (Luke 24:1-12).

Introduction

Luke the beloved physician (Colossians 4:14) is regarded as one of the world's great historians. In both the twenty four chapters of his carefully written Gospel, and in his meticulously written, twenty eight chaptered history of the spread and triumph of the Gospel in the first century, Graeco-Roman world - the Acts of the Apostles - Luke's emphasis is that Jesus is the divine Saviour that we so desperately need.

When Jesus was born in Bethlehem, Luke records the Good News that was literally sent from heaven so: *to you is born this day in the city of David a Saviour Who is Christ the Lord* (Luke 2:11). In Luke 15:2, Luke records that the enemies of Jesus made the following remark: *'This Man receives sinners and eats with them.'* And in perhaps the key verse of Luke - Luke 19:10 - quoting words from the lips of the Saviour Himself, we are told *'The Son of Man came to seek and to save the lost.*

The living, life-giving Saviour

It stands to reason that a dead Saviour is powerless to save. In 1 Corinthians 15:17, Luke's friend, Paul, put it bluntly: *If Christ has not been raised, your faith is futile and you are still in your sins.* Luke, however, *having followed all things closely* (Luke 1:3) and undertaken the most careful, scientific research, believed adamantly in both a living and a life-giving Saviour. In his book, Luke records that the same Christ Who was crucified on Good Friday was also raised from the dead on Easter Sunday. When Luke was undertaking his research and gathering his evidence, he found it so compelling that he felt forced to write it down and make *an orderly account* (Luke 1:3) of it all. Under the inspiration of the Holy Spirit then, here is Luke's written testimony to the risen Saviour - a testimony independent of Matthew, Mark and John's testimony. It is similar to theirs and yet different from theirs, thus adding another facet to Christ's resurrection. All in all though, Luke would have given a resounding 'Amen!' to Hebrews 7:25: *He is able for all time to save those who draw near to God through Him, since He always lives to make intercession for them.*

Taking us back to the first Easter morning, Luke begins with:-

1. The Day

On the *first day* of the week . . .(v.1). The 'first day' of the week here, refers to the day after the Jewish Sabbath - our

Sunday. This day was to become the Christian Sabbath, a day specially set aside for worship and fellowship. In this we have some indirect, but no less compelling, evidence for the resurrection of Christ. It is almost inconceivable that the sacred Jewish Sabbath day could ever be changed. To do so would be a blatant violation of the fourth commandment: *Remember the Sabbath day to keep it holy . . . the seventh day is a Sabbath to the LORD your God . . .* (Exodus 20:8 ff.). Since the first century Christians have kept the first day, not the seventh day of the week, as the weekly Sabbath. Only the fact that Christ was raised from the dead on this day can account for such a major, epochal change.

 On the first day of the week . . . The day was a 'first' in every way:-

 On the very first day ever, the Bible records *God said 'Let there be light'; and there was light* (Genesis 1:3). 2 Timothy 1:10 reveals that *our Saviour Christ Jesus . . . abolished death and brought life and immortality to light through the Gospel.* Acts 26:23 tells us that *Christ . . . being the first to rise from the dead . . . would proclaim light both to the people and to the Gentiles.* Colossians 1:18 describes Christ as *the first-born from the dead.* This all just would not be so if it were not for the events of this *first day of the week* - the first Easter morning when *God raised Him from the dead* (Acts 13:30).

 The majority in Jerusalem were no doubt pleasantly asleep at this moment - unconscious and unaware that they were sleeping through the dawning of the greatest and most momentous day that this world has ever known to date:-

Blest morning, whose first dawning rays
Beheld the Son of God
Arise triumphant from the grave
And leave His dark abode

Wrapt in the silence of the tomb
The great Redeemer lay
Till the revolving skies had brought
The third, the appointed day

Hell and the grave combined their force
To hold our Lord, in vain
Sudden the Conqueror arose
And burst their feeble chain.

Day however, begins with:-

2. The Dawn

*On the first day of the week, at early dawn, they (the women)
went to the tomb . . .* (v.1).

John's account differs from Luke's here. He says *Now on
the first day of the week Mary Magdalene came to the tomb early,
while it was still dark* (John 20:1). There is no contradiction between the two accounts though. They are easily reconciled if
we imagine, in our mind's eye, Mary Magdalene and the others
leaving their lodgings in the dark and arriving at the tomb in
the dawn light, just as the day was breaking.

We have here then a new dawn and a new day in every
sense. Dawn speaks of hope. The darkness has ended and the
light is here! The dawning of the day is a rich Scriptural meditation for us:- *weeping may tarry for the night, but joy comes with the
morning* (Psalm 30:5). *The steadfast love of the LORD never ceases,
His mercies never come to an end; they are new every morning; great
is Thy faithfulness* (Lamentations 3:22,23).

Getting out of bed before anyone else though, tells us a
lot about these women's devotion. The desire of their minds
was stronger than the comfort of their mattresses!

3. The Devotion

*. . . they went to the tomb, taking the spices which they had
prepared* (v.1). The 'they' here is explained in Luke 23:55 as referring to *The women who had come with Him from Galilee.* Verse 10
of our chapter names these women as *Mary Magdalene and Joanna
and Mary the mother of James and the other women with them . . .*

Whatever else was or was not true of these women, their devotion to the Saviour stands out. We have to admit that their devotion puts the disciples' devotion - or lack of it - to shame. The disciples were nowhere to be seen. These women's affection and respect for the Saviour though saw them making some personal sacrifices, and gladly so. At a cost to themselves they, seeing *the tomb, and how His body was laid . . . returned, and prepared spices and ointments* (Luke 23:55,56). Now, with the Jewish Sabbath over, *they went to the tomb, taking the spices which they had prepared.* Their intention, on that Sunday morning, was to perform one last act of devotion to the Saviour - and their devotion was to be well rewarded. Honouring Jesus and honouring God are actually the same thing, for *He who confesses the Son has the Father also* (1 John 2:23). In Samuel's day, God said *those who honour Me, I will honour* (1 Samuel 2:30). These women honoured Christ, and God in turn honoured them, making them the first witnesses of the empty tomb, as well as giving them an honourable place in His Book, the Bible - the Word of God which abides for ever. Oh to emulate something of the spirit of these women's devotion!

> Myrrh and spices will I bring
> True affection's offering
> Close the door from sight and sound
> Of the busy world around
> And in patient watch remain
> Till my Lord appear again.

Devotion to Jesus does not happen in a vacuum. Devotion is a practical expression of gratitude. Mary Magdalene here, for example, was supremely grateful to Jesus because He had transformed her life. Luke 8:3 tells us that Jesus had cast seven demons out of her. It goes to show that we will only truly serve Jesus when we have first been served by Him. We will only give to Him when we have first received from Him. Salvation is all of grace, and service is all of gratitude. The principle runs throughout the New Testament. Luke 7:36, to take another case, exemplifies another woman who loved Jesus because Jesus had forgiven her all her sins. Her devotion to Him was similarly lavish in response. Jesus explained: *'I tell you, her sins, which are many, are forgiven, for she loved much; but he who is forgiven little, loves little* (Luke 7:47). The Apostle John taught in a similar vein, years later, when he wrote *We love because He first loved us* (1 John 4:19). Devotion to Jesus therefore is caused and fuelled, not by music, 'atmosphere', 'visual aids' or by working ourselves up into an emotional state. No. Devotion to Jesus results from being a recipient of His favour, and a true meditation and understanding of all that He has done for us.

The women's devotion here was certainly sincere. Yet the women's devotion was sincerely misguided! They wanted to anoint Jesus's dead body - but there was actually no dead body to anoint. Christ had risen. Their devotion now was instrumental in leading them to make the greatest discovery of all time:-

4. The Discovery

And they found the stone rolled away from the tomb, but when they went in they did not find the body of the Lord Jesus (vv.2,3).

The resurrection of the Lord Jesus Christ has been well termed 'the most attested fact in history.' The transformation of the disciples, the change of the Sabbath day, the growth of the Christian church, not to mention the individual experience of Christian salvation, just cannot be explained apart from the literal, historical truth of Christ's bodily resurrection. These, however, may be described as the 'consequential' evidence for Christ's resurrection. The primary evidence for Christ's resurrection, according to the Gospel records, is twofold. The evidence is composite, for sure, yet the evidence may be pared down to two stubborn facts which cannot be explained away. The facts are these: i. Joseph's tomb was empty of Christ's body. ii. The risen Christ appeared to various people, on various occasions. We are concerned here with the first fact - the fact that Joseph of Arimathea's tomb was empty on the first Easter morning. Christ had vacated the tomb. The stone was now rolled away. It was rolled away, not so much to let Christ out - for elsewhere we see that Christ now had the ability to appear and disappear through walls at will - as to let the eyewitnesses in to see the evidence for themselves. Let us compare and contrast what Luke says about Good Friday and Easter Sunday:-

i. On Good Friday: Joseph *asked for the body of Jesus. Then he took it down and wrapped it in a linen shroud, and laid Him in a rock-hewn tomb where no one had ever yet been laid* (Luke 23:52,53). *The women who had come with Him from Galilee followed, and saw the tomb, and how His body was laid* (Luke 23:55).

ii. On Easter Sunday, these same women *went to the tomb . . . And they found the stone rolled away from the tomb, but when they went in* they did not find the body (vv.1-3).

The tomb was empty, for Christ had risen. In the days and weeks and months after, when the message of Christ's resurrection was proclaimed with such fervour, if Christ had not actually been raised from the dead, it would have been the simplest thing to produce His body, and thus refute the Church's claim, exposing it as a fraud once and for all. This though was never done. It was never done because it could not be done, for Christ had risen from the dead.

> Death could not keep its prey
> Jesus, my Saviour!
> He tore the bars away
> Jesus, my Lord!
>
> Up from the grave He arose
> With a mighty triumph o'er His foes
> He arose a Victor o'er the dark domain
> And He lives for ever with His saints to reign!
> He arose! He arose!
> Hallelujah! Christ arose!

Christ's resurrected body had most certainly vacated the tomb. Yet paradoxically the tomb was still occupied. Luke records that two angelic beings were there - angels who had an amazing declaration to make concerning the Christ Whom the women thought was dead for good.

5. The Dazzlers

. . . when they went in . . . they did not find the body. While they were perplexed about this, behold, two men stood by them in dazzling apparel; . . . they (the women) were frightened and bowed their faces to the ground (vv.3-5).

The reaction of the women to the supernatural was a natural one. We would have done the same in the unexpected presence of two dazzling angels. Luke mentions that there were two angels at the empty tomb. John's account agrees with Luke here (see John 20:12). The fact that Matthew and Mark only mention one angel is not a contradiction. It is explained by Matthew and Mark focusing solely on the angel who was the spokesman for the two. These apparent differences in the evidence given by the four Gospel writers though actually confirm the truth of their overall story, and the independence of their four written testimonies and standpoints. John Wenham puts it this way

> The resurrection stories exhibit in a remarkable way the well-known characteristics of accurate and independent reporting, for superficially they show great disharmony, but on close examination the details gradually fall into place (*Easter Enigma* p.11).

Similarly, of the apparent contradictions between the four Gospel accounts of Christ's resurrection, Donald Bridge makes the pointed comment:-

> (The apparent contradictions are) an argument in favour of the basic

truthfulness of the varied stories.
Every policeman and magistrate can
smell a cooked-up tale. One sure sign
of it is total agreement between pro-
fessedly independent witnesses.
Genuine witnesses will often sound
contradictory, simply because each
has a partial experience and knowledge, and each tells it from a different standpoint. . . . Conversely, a false
agreed alibi or conspiracy will sound
plausible on the surface, but begins
to crumble during an in-depth inter-
rogation (*Jesus - The Man and His Message*, p.142).

The heavenly messengers though had something to say.
Their message was two-fold. First of all they had a negative
denouncement, and secondly, a positive declaration.

6. The Denouncement

'Why do you seek the living among the dead?' (v.5).

We have here a gentle rebuke. The women had got it
wrong. Although they meant well, looking for a living Saviour
at a place for the dead was both literally and metaphorically a
grave error. They had to be rebuked for this: *'Why do you seek the
living among the dead? He is not here, but has risen.'*
Religions and Faiths other than Christianity have their
revered founders too. The very keen may pay homage to the
earthly remains of such and visit their graves. It is here that the
Christian Faith is infinitely different. We cannot pay our respects
to Christ's dead bones, for He is alive. *God raised Him up, having
loosed the pangs of death, because it was not possible for Him to be
held by it* (Acts 2:24). Christ is both a living and a life-giving
Saviour. He can still say to His Own *'Fear not, I am the first and*

the last and the <u>living One</u>; I died and behold I am alive for evermore, and I have the keys of death and Hades' (Revelation 1:17,18). Christian testimony in the twenty first century AD is identical to that of Job, two thousand years BC. *I know that my Redeemer lives* (Job 19:25). Next, the angels went on to remind the women - and, by implication, us - of some basic fundamentals of the Christian Faith:-

7. The Declaration

'Remember how He told you, while He was still in Galilee, that the Son of Man must be delivered into the hands of sinful men, and be crucified, and on the third day rise.' And they remembered His words (vv. 7,8).

At the angel's declaration, 'the penny dropped.' The women remembered the words of Jesus. They now understood that the death and resurrection of Jesus was no accident but an appointment. It was all according to God's plan of redemption. The women recalled how Christ Himself had foretold His death and resurrection whilst they followed Him in Galilee. Unpacking this angelic declaration, we note:-

i. The death and resurrection of Christ was all according to prophecy

'Remember how He told you ... Christ had indeed predicted His Own death and resurrection, as indeed had the Old Testament Scriptures before His time on earth. Somehow though, these predictions were lost on His followers. It is difficult for us to understand how this was so, but with our unfair advantage of two thousand years of New Testament hindsight, we should not be too critical.

The events surrounding both the cross and the empty tomb were all according to the Divine plan of salvation. Jesus, being so integral to the Divine plan of salvation, and being so 'privy' to it, was able to explain to His followers the exact details of these saving events long before they actually happened. Luke recorded some of His prophecies in his Gospel:-

*'The Son of Man must suffer many things, and be rejected by
the elders and chief priests, and be killed, and on the third day be raised'*
(Luke 9:22). Similarly, in Luke 18:31 ff., we read of Jesus's pre-
diction: *And taking the twelve, He said to them, 'Behold, we are going up to Jerusalem, and everything that is written of the Son of Man
by the prophets will be accomplished. For He will be delivered to the
Gentiles, and will be mocked and shamefully treated and spit upon;
they will scourge Him and kill Him, and on the third day He will rise.'*

ii. The death and resurrection of Christ was an absolute necessity

*Remember how He told you . . . that the Son of Man <u>must</u> . . . be
crucified . . . and rise.* The word 'must' here carries the meaning
of 'absolutely necessary' and 'totally binding.' The word shows
that the death and resurrection of Christ were absolutely necessary to procure our salvation. Nothing else would suffice. There
was no other way. The Good News though is that Christ did
actually go on to die and rise again. As the hymn says: 'the pain
that He endured, our salvation hath procured.' Christ alone
could pay the wages of our sin. Christ alone could offer a sinless,
spotless sacrifice to appease the wrath of God. The death of
Christ alone - in His Person as the Son of God - is sufficient to
save eternally. The empty tomb is evidence of God's total pleas-
ure and satisfaction with the saving sacrifice that Christ made.
His death really does atone for sin. The empty tomb proves it.
Put negatively, *If Christ has not been raised . . . you are still in your
sins . . . But in fact Christ has been raised from the dead* (1 Corinthians
15:17,20).

We cannot, therefore, get more fundamental than the cross
and the empty tomb. Prophecy predicted them. The sin of man
and the justice of God required them. The believing soul em-
braces them and rejoices in them, and appreciates the blessings
which flow from them, both now and eternally:-

Ye mortals, catch the sound
Redeemed by Him from Hell
And send the echo round
The globe on which you dwell
Transported, cry
'Jesus, Who bled
Hath left the dead
No more to die.'

Good News is for sharing. This being so, the women felt an inner compulsion to tell the disciples that their best Friend was not in fact dead after all:-

8. The Disciples

and returning from the tomb they told all this to the eleven and to the rest (v.9).

The evidence for Christ's resurrection is cumulative. Every effect has a cause. It was the Good News of Christ's resurrection that caused the women to seek the remaining disciples of Jesus. Their behaviour is inexplicable otherwise. They had something earth shattering to share, so off they went to the remaining eleven disciples.

Christ originally chose twelve disciples. On a sadder, sobering point, we note that there are only eleven disciples now. The number twelve reminds us of the twelve tribes of Israel, showing again that in the Christian Faith we have the fulfilment of the many promises which God made in the Old Testament. Now though there are only eleven disciples, for Judas Iscariot, having betrayed the Lord Jesus, was unable to live with himself, and went and took his own life. If one of Jesus's specially chosen disciples could fall so tragically, what about us? How imperative it is that we seek to maintain a constant and consistent close fellowship with God. Watchfulness is a lesser known Christian virtue, outwardly unspectacular, but nonetheless vital. This being said though, ultimately, we do not keep ourselves. God does. *Now to Him Who is able to keep you from falling and to present you without blemish before the presence of His glory with rejoicing* (Jude 24).

Finally, what of the reaction of the disciples to the amazing news which the women brought them? Surely Luke is going to build up to a crescendo and go on to describe one of the greatest praise services ever? Surprisingly, he does not. The women were actually met by disbelief:-

9. The Disbelief

When the women *told this to the apostles . . . .*says Luke *these words seemed to them an idle tale, and they did not believe them* (v.11).

What a way to finish your account of the first Easter morning. Luke ends by telling us of the disciples' unbelief. Here again, in this picture of the disciples 'warts and all', we have yet more evidence that Luke's account is fact and not fiction. Here we have sane and sober history, not some carefully concocted creativity. No one would or could have thought of inventing an ending like this.

Initially then, the disciples viewed the report of Christ's resurrection as *an idle tale . . . they did not believe. . .* It was to take the personal appearance of the risen Christ to convince them otherwise and transform them into ambassadors of the Same. We wonder though how they reacted when people refused to believe their message . . .

And so we leave Luke's account of the first Easter morning. Throughout, it has born the marks of total integrity and veracity. It has the ring of truth running right through it. Luke has shown that the crucified Saviour is the conquering Saviour. The Christ Who was crucified and buried also conquered the grave three days later.

Up from the grave He arose
With a mighty triumph o'er His foes
He arose, a Victor from the dark domain
And He lives for ever with His saints to reign
He arose! He arose!
Hallelujah! Christ arose!

Chapter 4

A Heart Warming Encounter on the Emmaus Road

That very day two of them were going to a village named Emmaus, about seven miles from Jerusalem, and talking with each other about all these things that had happened. While they were talking and discussing together, Jesus Himself drew near and went with them. But their eyes were kept from recognising Him. And He said to them, 'What is this conversation which you are holding with each other as you walk?' And they stood still, looking sad. Then one of them, named Cleopas, answered Him, 'Are you the only visitor to Jerusalem who does not know the things that have happened there in these days?' And He said to them, 'What things?' And they said to Him, 'Concerning Jesus of Nazareth, Who was a prophet mighty in deed and word before God and all the people, and how our chief priests and rulers delivered Him up to be condemned to death, and crucified Him. But we had hoped that He was the One to redeem Israel. Yes, and besides all this, it is now the third day since this happened. Moreover, some women of our company amazed us. They were at the tomb early in the morning and did not find His body; and they came back saying that they had even seen a vision of angels, who said that He was alive. Some of those who were with us went to the tomb, and found it just as the women had said; but Him they did not see.' And He said to them, 'O foolish men, and slow of heart to believe all that the prophets have spoken! Was it not necessary that the Christ should suffer these things and enter into His glory?' And beginning with Moses and all the prophets, He interpreted to them in all the Scriptures the things concerning Himself.

So they drew near to the village to which they were going. He appeared to be going further, but they constrained Him, saying, 'Stay with us, for it is toward evening and the day is now far spent.' So He went in to stay with them. When He was at table with them, He took the bread and blessed, and broke it, and gave it to them. And their eyes were opened and they recognised Him; and He vanished out of their sight. They said to each other, 'Did not our hearts burn within us while He talked to us on the road, while He opened to us the Scriptures?' And they rose that same hour and returned to Jerusalem; and they found the eleven gathered together and those who were with them, who said, 'The Lord has risen indeed, and has appeared to Simon!' Then they told what had happened on the road, and how He was known to them in the breaking of the bread (Luke 24: 13-35).

Introduction

During the afternoon of the first Easter Sunday, two of the Lord Jesus's followers made their way on foot from Jerusalem to Emmaus. Emmaus is a village about seven miles north west of Jerusalem. As they walked, the condition of their hearts was very heavy and sad, because they were convinced that the Lord Jesus was dead. Unbeknown to them though, Christ had risen from the dead. On that Emmaus road, they were to have a heart warming encounter with the risen Saviour, for *While they were talking and discussing together JESUS HIMSELF DREW NEAR and went with them* (Luke 24:15):-

Jesus Himself drew near
And joined them as they walked
And soon their hearts began to burn
As of Himself He talked

Jesus Himself drew near
They were no longer sad

When He was walking at their side
How could they but be glad?

Jesus Himself drew near
And all their doubts were solved
He showed them why He came to die
And what that death involved

Jesus Himself drew near
And at the journey's end
They could not let Him leave them thus
The stranger was their Friend.

Mark 16:12 tells us that Jesus *appeared in another form to two of them, as they were walking into the country.* We cannot say for certain whether these two are the same two as here. We can say, however, that this detailed account of the Emmaus road walk is unique to Luke's Gospel. He alone recorded it for posterity, and how grateful we are that he did. The story of the Emmaus road is a wonderful story, for in it we see some ordinary people whose needs were met in Christ, and in doing so, we witness an eternal principle: On the one hand we have men and women in their need, and on the other hand we have God's answer to our need. God's answer to our need is the living Christ of the Scriptures, as we shall see now as we consider the account a little more closely.

1. The Trudge

Emmaus, then, was about seven miles from Jerusalem. In normal health, walking at about three and a half miles per hour, such a walk would take about two hours. Our mental state though can make a distance seem longer and our walk slower. Mental and psychological burdens can weigh us down as much as physical ones. As the two walkers here went on their way, they walked with burdened steps. They were downcast, disappointed, disheartened, discouraged, despondent, and even a little depressed. At one point *they stood still looking sad* (v.17). Why? Because they mistakenly thought that they had lost their best Friend for ever: *'concerning Jesus of Nazareth Who was a prophet mighty in deed and word before God and all the people . . . our chief priests and rulers delivered Him up to be condemned to death and crucified Him'* (vv.19,20). Believing that Jesus was now gone, their hope had likewise gone: *'we had hoped that He was the One to redeem Israel '*(v.21). The walkers were definitely sincere in their sorrow - even if they were sincerely wrong!

Luke's Gospel has an interesting contrast here. In Luke 2: 41 ff., we can read of some walkers from Jerusalem who mistakenly thought that Jesus was with them when He actually was not with them. Here on the Emmaus road though, we have some walkers from Jerusalem who mistakenly thought that Jesus was not with them when He actually was with them.

They stood still looking sad . . . we had hoped that He was the One to redeem Israel. Such was the sad state of these two walkers when the risen Saviour drew near to them. They did not, as yet, believe in the resurrection of Christ. Jesus's own words which prophesied His rising from the dead on the third day, somehow had not rubbed off on them. *'besides all this, it is now the third day since this happened . . .'* (v.21). They did not believe the reports even, so fast stuck were they in their downcast frame of mind. Their initial scepticism comes through clearly here: *'some women of our company amazed us. They were at the tomb early in the morning and did not find His body . . . they came back saying that they had even seen a vision of angels, who said that He was alive. Some of those who were with us went to the tomb, and found it just as the women had said, but Him they did not see . . . '*(v. 22 ff.).

Before we are too harsh on these two walkers, let us try and understand them. They did not, as yet, believe that Christ had risen from the dead. The whole Christian Faith though stands or falls on Christ's resurrection. If Christ's resurrection is not true, then the whole Faith is untrue. A dead Saviour is powerless to save. Paul put it like this: *If Christ has not been raised then our preaching is in vain and your faith is in vain* (1 Corinthians 15:14). *If Christ has not been raised, your faith is futile and you are still in your sins. Then those also who have fallen asleep in Christ have perished. If for this life only we have hoped in Christ, we are of all men most to be pitied* (1 Corinthians 15:17-19).

Cleopas and his friend had very heavy hearts as they trudged the seven miles to Emmaus. This was how they were when they encountered the risen Christ!

2. The Teacher

The two disciples thought that Jesus was dead, and hence their sorrow. But *Jesus Himself drew near.* Luke then records, rather strangely, *But their eyes were kept from recognising Him* (v.16).

The question is asked: Why did Jesus not reveal Himself to them immediately? Why did He keep the veil over their eyes? The answer is, that the greatest Teacher of all time wanted to give them the greatest Bible study of all time, so that the truth of God would be ingrained into their hearts:-

Cleopas was sad because *the chief priests and rulers (had) delivered Him (Jesus) up to be condemned to death and crucified.* The risen Saviour though wanted to teach him that the cause of his current sadness was actually all part of the Divine plan. Tragic though the crucifixion seemed, it was all according to God's Word as revealed in the Scriptures. In fact, the very events of Calvary which caused Cleopas to be so down cast, were the very events which were necessary to procure the salvation of God's people. And so the Lord had to utter a gentle rebuke: '*O foolish men and slow of heart to believe all that the prophets have spoken! Was it not necessary that the Christ should suffer these things and enter into His glory?* (vv.25,26). And to prove His point, the world's greatest Teacher proceeded to give them the greatest Bible study of all time. *And beginning with Moses and all the prophets, He interpreted to them in all the Scriptures the things concerning Himself* (v.27). Christ showed the necessity of Calvary according to the Scriptures:-

Oh what a Bible study have we here
Not barren theory - musty, dry and drear

> But Christ, the 'altogether lovely', full in view
> Himself the preacher, text and sermon too.

The Greatest Bible Study Ever

In this greatest Bible study ever, we have:-
i. The Greatest Teacher - the Lord Jesus Christ, Who is truth incarnate.
ii. The Greatest Textbook - the Bible, God's inspired Word.
iii. The Greatest Theme - i.e. *the things concerning* Christ Himself: His superlative Person and His saving work on the Cross.

What a Bible study therefore this was. It informed the mind, it fed the soul and it warmed the heart: *Did not our hearts burn within us while He talked to us on the road, while He opened to us the Scriptures ?* (v.32). How we wish we could have tuned in! The Bible is silent to its exact contents though. We can say though that it must have been a bird's-eye study, rather than an in-depth study - telescopic rather than microscopic - as all the Scriptures could not be studied in depth in such a short time. We can only speculate as to what the Saviour actually taught. But Christ is clearly revealed in *Moses and all the prophets* for sure. Consider *Moses*:-

Perhaps He mentioned the first ever promise of redemption in the Bible, the so called 'proto euangelion' of Genesis 3:15. Here, at the dawn of history, God promised that the coming seed of the woman would one day come and crush Satan's head. He would deal him a crushing blow, whilst being bruised Himself in the process.

Surely Christ spoke of the Passover Lamb of Exodus 12 - the Lamb which was slain, and whose blood was shed and applied to bring deliverance from the angel of death.

Surely Christ mentioned the Day of Atonement in Leviticus 16. Here, in the scape-goat who bears away the sins of the people, we have a clear picture of Christ.

Did Christ mention the bronze serpent of Numbers 21 in His Bible study? When this snake was lifted up, the people looked to it and were healed instantly. Christ Himself was also lifted up, and those who look to Him are eternally saved.

Moses certainly spoke of Christ, but so did *all the prophets* :-

To take just one. What of Isaiah 53? Who can this refer to but Christ? *He was wounded for our transgressions, He was bruised for our iniquities* (Isaiah 53:5).

If we open the Bible anywhere, we will find Christ somewhere, for Christ is the key to the Scriptures. Cleopas and his companion were shown the centrality of Scripture, the centrality of Christ in Scripture, and the centrality of the death of Christ in all the Scriptures. The incarnate Word interpreted the inspired Word in that greatest Bible study of all time. On the Emmaus road, the living Word brought the written Word to life. Beyond the sacred page, they met the Lord. Although a crucified Saviour was initially something of a puzzle to Cleopas, Christ put him right -and he put him right from the Scriptures. *The prophets . . . predicting the suffering of Christ and the subsequent glory* (1 Peter 1:10). *Christ died for our sins in accordance with the Scriptures* (1 Corinthians 15:3).

3. The Testimony

The two walkers were absolutely enthralled by both the Word of God and the God of the Word. Naturally, they wished to cherish the moment for as long as they could. *So they drew near to the village to which they were going. He appeared to be going further, but they constrained Him saying 'Stay with us, for it is toward evening and the day is now far spent . . .'* (v.29). As an aside, we note that it is this verse which gave rise to one of the English speaking world's most well loved hymns. *'Stay with us, for it is toward evening . . .*

Abide with me, fast falls the eventide
The darkness deepens, Lord with me abide
When other helpers fail and comforts flee
Help of the helpless, O abide with me.

Graciously, the Lord Jesus complied with their request. *So He went in to stay with them* (v.29). It is now that the narrative reaches its culmination and climax, for Luke records *When He was at table with them, He took the bread and blessed and broke it and gave it to them. AND THEIR EYES WERE OPENED AND THEY RECOGNISED HIM and He vanished out of their sight* (v.30 ff.).

Unusually, the special Guest became the special Host: *He took the bread and blessed and broke it and gave it to them.* Did they see the marks of Calvary as He took the bread - those nail pierced hands which had wrought redemption? Did they recall the feeding of the five thousand, when the Saviour likewise 'took, blessed, broke and gave'? Did they even think of the Lord's Supper? There, in the Upper Room, the Lord also 'took, blessed, broke and gave'? Whatever the case was, *THEIR EYES WERE OPENED AND THEY RECOGNISED HIM.*

He lives! He lives! Christ Jesus lives today
He walks with me and He talks with me, along life's narrow way.

But in fact Christ has been raised from the dead, the first fruits of those who have fallen asleep. For as by a man came death, by a Man has come also the resurrection of the dead (1 Corinthians 15:20 ff.).

Interestingly, the account of the Emmaus road contains two 'open things':-

i. *He opened to us the Scriptures* (v.32)

ii. *Their eyes were opened and they recognised Him* (v.32).

The latter is the climax of the whole incident we are studying. It was the moment of the two walkers' personal salvation. They, along with every true believer, could now truly sing:-

I know that my Redeemer lives
What joy the blest assurance gives!
He lives, He lives Who once was dead
He lives my everlasting Head

He lives triumphant from the grave
He lives eternally to save
He lives all glorious in the sky
He lives exalted there on high

He lives to bless me with His love
And still for me He pleads above
He lives to raise me from the grave
And me eternally to save.

What a testimony these walkers now had to tell. A wonderful change had been wrought in their lives, and they gave evidence of their salvation. One evidence of salvation is the desire to tell others - to share our knowledge of the risen Saviour with one and all. This being so *they rose that same hour and returned to Jerusalem, and found the eleven gathered together and those who were with them* (v.33). Remember that they had already trudged this seven mile road once. Now they were retracing their steps, and that without a trace of fatigue. What a contrast there was between now and their first journey. Then, they trudged despondently, now they had a spring in their step, a song in their heart and great joy in their souls.

4. The Triumph

The two hurried back from Emmaus to Jerusalem to tell their friends the Good News. But their friends got their word in first. Before the two could speak, their friends spoke. They too knew that Christ had risen. *They found the eleven gathered together and those who were with them who said 'The Lord has risen indeed and has appeared to Simon'* (vv.33,34). The Lord has risen indeed! Here we have the Church's song of triumph. At Easter time, the following liturgy is used in some churches. The verse and response goes back to the very early Church:-

'Alleluia, Christ has risen.'
'He is risen indeed, Alleluia.'

The Lord has risen indeed.

> The Lord is risen indeed
> And are the tidings true?
> Yes, they beheld the Saviour bleed
> And saw Him risen too
>
> The Lord is risen indeed
> Then is His work performed
> The captive Surety now is freed
> And death, our foe disarmed
>
> The Lord is risen indeed
> He lives to die no more
> He lives the sinner's cause to plead
> Whose curse and shame He bore.

Finally, noticing a small detail which would be easy to overlook, we note:-

5. The Tenderness

'The Lord has risen indeed and has appeared to <u>*Simon*</u> (v.34).

The Simon referred to here is better known as Simon Peter. Simon Peter, interestingly, figures prominently in relation to the Lord's resurrection:-

'Do not be amazed; you seek Jesus of Nazareth, Who was crucified. He has risen, He is not here; see the place where they laid Him. But go, tell His disciples AND PETER that He is going before you to Galilee . . . (Mark 16:6,7).

And in the earliest resurrection account of all, we see how:-

He was raised on the third day in accordance with the Scriptures and that He appeared to CEPHAS (i.e. Peter), then to the twelve (1 Corinthians 15:4,5).

Peter was certainly in need of special care and personal assurance - and he received it. In a moment of weakness and cowardice, Peter had denied His Master three times. His consequent sorrow and remorse were almost unbearable. He had failed abysmally. Perhaps he thought that he had condemned himself to be a failure for ever, and that there was now no hope for him, and no more earthly use for him . . . But all was not lost. There was restorative grace with the living Saviour. Peter was yet to be used in the purposes of God, and that in a mighty way. The risen Saviour thus *appeared to Simon*. He appeared to him privately, and restored him to Himself. Scripture does not allow us in on this very tender moment, yet the fact that it happened at all gives us all hope. *He restores my soul* (Psalm 23:3). *A bruised reed He will not break, and a dimly burning wick He will not quench* (Isaiah 42:3).

George Whitefield, the great eighteenth century preacher, used to say words to the effect that 'The Christian life is a series of new starts.' Without excusing our shameful faults and failures, it is good to know that there is mercy with the Lord. He is merciful to those who turn to Him, and He is merciful to those who return to Him. *If we say we have no sin we deceive ourselves and the truth is not in us. If we confess our sins He is faithful and just and will forgive our sins and cleanse us from all unrighteousness* (1 John 1:8,9).

Luke's Gospel in general is a Gospel of hope. In it we see the compassionate Son of Man Who came to seek and to save the lost. Luke shows Jesus to be the tender Saviour of sinners. He died for our sins and was raised from the dead and is able to save to the uttermost all those who come to God by Him. In Luke's account of the road to Emmaus, we see a Saviour Who meets us on the way - a Saviour Who is the answer to our every need.

Chapter Five

John's Account of the First Easter Sunday

PART I: THE EMPTY TOMB

Introduction

Whilst an open minded reading of any of the Gospel accounts will convince us of the Deity of Christ - that is, that Jesus Christ is God - this is especially true of John's Gospel. John's Gospel's peculiar and particular perspective is that of the total and absolute 'God-ness' of Christ. It leads the reader, with Thomas, to confess of Christ : *'My Lord and my God'* (John 20:28).

John opens his Gospel by explaining of Christ *In the beginning was the Word, and the Word was with God, and the Word was God* (John 1:1), and if we open the twenty one chapters which follow anywhere, we will find Christ's deity somewhere. His works and words betray Him. The evidence for Christ's deity is all unmistakably there in John's Gospel, and this is especially the case in John's account of the first Easter morning, where he records how Christ conquered the grave and so was *designated Son of God in power according to the Spirit of holiness by His resurrection from the dead* (Romans 1:4). Christ's resurrection is indeed the keystone in the evidence which proves His deity - as well as the capstone and foundation stone of the glorious arch which is the Christian Faith.

The evidence which John gives to prove that Jesus really did have power to lay down His life and have power to take it again (c.f. John 10:18) is manifold and cumulative. We have summarised it however in a twofold way. There is the evidence of i. The empty tomb and ii. the appearances of the risen Christ. We will deal with John's account of the empty tomb now, and then consider John's accounts of the personal appearances of the risen Christ in the chapters which follow.

John's account of the empty tomb on the first Easter morning

Now on the first day of the week Mary Magdalene came to the tomb early, while it was still dark, and saw that the stone had been taken away from the tomb. So she ran, and went to Simon Peter and the other disciple, the one whom Jesus loved, and said to them, 'They have taken the Lord out of the tomb, and we do not know where they have laid Him.' Peter then came out with the other disciple, and they went toward the tomb. They both ran, but the other disciple outran Peter and reached the tomb first; and stooping to look in, he saw the linen cloths lying there, but he did not go in. Then Simon Peter came, following him, and went into the tomb; he saw the linen cloths lying, and the napkin, which had been on His head, not lying with the linen cloths but rolled up in a place by itself. Then the other disciple, who reached the tomb first, also went in, and he saw and believed; for as yet they did not know the Scripture, that He must rise from the dead. Then the disciples went back to their homes (John 20:1-10).

Having read John's account of the empty tomb, we are immediately struck by its vividness. The only way of accounting for this graphic vividness is to say that it is the product of John's personal memory. After all, he was there and he knew all the people involved. Those who propound that the apostle John is not actually the author of John's Gospel, propose a difficult, even untenable theory, which makes far more difficulties than it solves.

Returning to the garden tomb outside Jerusalem's walls though, very early on the first Easter Sunday, we note some of the various activities going on:-

1. Visiting

> *Mary Magdalene came to the tomb early, . . . and saw that the stone had been taken away* (v.1).

Aware of her infinite debt to the grace of the Lord and Lord of all grace, Mary ensured that she was the first to the Lord's tomb on the first Easter day. (The 'we' of v.2 however shows that she was followed and accompanied by the other women - as we have seen in the previous accounts.)

Mary, then, sought the Lord. Proverbs 8:17 may be applied fittingly to her: *I love those who love Me , and those who seek Me diligently find Me.* Her love for the Lord saw her seeking Him early. We note once again though, that any thought of the Lord's resurrection was far from her mind. Her visit was for the purpose of revering a dead Person and paying her last respects.

John's account suggests here that Mary's devotion was such that she associated the body of the Lord with the Lord Himself. In her confusion, seeing that the grave stone had been taken away, she feared grave robbers had been at work in the night. She did not, however say 'They have stolen the Lord's body' but *They have taken away the Lord* (v.2). Seeing that the grave had been disturbed, and fearing the worst, lead to:-

2. Hurrying

> *So she ran, and went to Simon Peter and the other disciple, the one whom Jesus loved, and said to them 'They have taken the Lord out of the tomb, and we do not know where they have laid Him'* (v.2).

i. *Simon Peter.* Judas Iscariot had betrayed the Lord, and in his remorse, went and committed suicide. Simon Peter had, in a moment of cowardice, denied the Lord three times . . . but here he was, still alive, and still associating himself with Jesus's disciples. Simon had been humbled right down, but he was still here. How do we account for this? Only by the power of Jesus's Own prayers for him. In Luke 22:31 ff. Jesus said *'Simon, Simon, behold, Satan demanded to have you, that He might sift you like wheat, but I have prayed for you that your faith may not fail . . .* Thank God for Jesus's prayers. It is they that keep us from failing shamefully and falling tragically. *He is able for all time to save those who draw near to God through Him since He always lives to make intercession for them* (Hebrews 7:25).

ii.*(John) - the other disciple, the one whom Jesus loved . . .* We know from John 19:26 ff. that John was looking after Mary, Jesus's earthly mother, now. At this very moment though, he too had no thought of ever seeing Jesus again. He was still, however, aware of the vast, infinite love that the Lord Jesus had for him. John's grief was the more acute because he had been so close to Jesus. At the Last Supper, he was even found *lying close to the breast of Jesus* (John 13:23).

3. Running

Mary's news of a possible grave disturbance - *'They have taken the Lord out of the tomb . . .'* - sprang Peter and John into action. They were in a hurry now too, and ran to the tomb as fast as they could. John, however, being younger and fitter than Peter, covered the ground more quickly: *Peter then came out with the other disciple, and they went toward the tomb. They both ran, but the other disciple outran Peter and reached the tomb first* (v.v.3,4). When they arrived at the tomb, puffing and panting, the concentration of their minds made them oblivious to any bodily discomfort. What had happened to the Lord? The disciples' minds were in overdrive.

4. Looking

Whilst John was the first to the tomb, he was the last into it. He showed a reverent restraint at barging into the place which supposedly held Jesus's earthly remains. John *reached the tomb first; and stooping to look in, he saw the linen cloths there, but he did not go in* (vv.4). Peter, however, reached the tomb last but entered it first. He had none of John's inhibitions. The impetuous, even bombastic nature of this former fisherman here is in line with his character throughout the New Testament. *Then Simon Peter came, following him (John), and went into the tomb* (v.6).

On entering the tomb, Peter saw the most remarkable sight - a sight which was subsequently to make such an impact on John, that it would not be too far-fetched to say that it was the transforming moment of his whole life. Years later, John, under the inspiration of the Holy Spirit, wrote down the details of what he saw in the tomb at this moment. He wrote down the details of the tomb's contents, so that we too may know and believe and be transformed by the truth of Jesus's resurrection. Notice the details of the tomb's contents which John describes - details which are unique to John's Gospel:-

5. Detailing

Simon Peter . . . went into the tomb; he saw the linen cloths lying, and the napkin which had been on His head, not lying with the linen cloths but rolled up in a place by itself (vv.6,7).

Despite Mary's initial fears, the contents of the tomb now before Peter's eyes showed that no grave robber had been at work. A grave robber would either have stolen the body completely, grave cloths and all, or else hurriedly and roughly ripped the body out of the bandages in which it was wrapped. The grave clothes however were completely intact. They had an orderly arrangement to them, just as they had when Jesus was buried - except now there was no body in them.

The only explanation of the grave clothes being left in such a way is that Jesus had passed through them miraculously! He had been raised, miraculously, from the dead. No human being was permitted to be there at the actual moment of Christ's resurrection, but the evidence of the grave clothes shows that the Lord Jesus, in resurrection power, passed right through His grave clothes. He then rolled up the napkin which covered His head, and left the tomb. Romans 6:9 comes to mind: *For we know that Christ being raised from the dead will never die again; death no longer has dominion over Him.*

John is silent as to Peter's initial reaction to all this. It was all so unexpected. Light and truth did not come to him immediately. Luke 24:12 says that *he went home wondering what had happened.* The same sight of the orderly grave clothes however had a much more immediate effect on John. Losing his initial diffidence, John too now went into the tomb. It was to lead to his:-

6. Believing

Then the other disciple, who reached the tomb first, also went in, and he saw and believed (v.8).

Here then is John's moment of moments - on a par with Paul's conversion experience on the Damascus Road, Luther's conversion experience in the University tower and Wesley's conversion experience in Aldgate Street. John, an intimate friend of the Lord Jesus, in seeing His empty, undisturbed grave clothes, just knew that Jesus had risen from the dead. The truth flooded his mind, inflamed his heart and saved his soul. John *saw and believed* - and he eventually wrote his experience down so that you and I might also be able to see and believe the same truth:-

Come, ye saints, look here and wonder
See the place where Jesus lay
He has burst His bands asunder
He has borne our sins away
Joyful tidings!
Yes, the Lord is risen today.

Believing, like John, that Jesus really did rise from the dead, is no mere academic matter. It is a vital matter. In fact, whether we believe this or not determines where we will spend eternity. Roman 10:9 says: *If you confess with your lips that Jesus is Lord and believe in your heart that God raised Him from the dead you will be saved.* GB Wilson comments on this verse:-

The part is put for the whole, for to
believe that 'God has raised Christ

from the dead, involves the belief that
Christ is all that He claimed to be, and
that He has accomplished all that He
came to perform'(Hodge).

John believed that Christ had risen from the dead, because
the empty grave clothes, there in front of him, completely intact, gave him no alternative - whilst Peter was to believe because he had a personal meeting with the risen Christ later. Both
John and Peter though, eventually, were to see that the Old Testament Scriptures had actually foretold Christ's resurrection. In
time, the Scriptures confirmed their belief, and they confirmed
their belief in the Scriptures. This gave them a great tool in their
evangelism - their proclaiming the risen Saviour to all and sundry. We have to say though, that their knowledge of the Scriptures at this moment was not what it would eventually be:-

7. Confirming

In due course, both John and Peter would realise that
Christ's resurrection, although unexpected by them, should actually have been expected by them. The resurrection was all
according to the will and plan and ordering of God, and already
made known by Him in His Word, the Scriptures. Just as the
day had now dawned, Scripture light eventually dawned on
Peter and John, but *as yet they did not know the Scripture that He
must rise from the dead* (v.9).

It was not long though before they became fully convinced of
the Scriptures concerning Christ's resurrection. Peter could write
many years later *we have the prophetic word made more sure* (2 Peter 1:19). Fifty days later, on the day of Pentecost, in his preaching, he proclaimed of Jesus *God raised Him up* (Acts 2:24) and
then went on to quote Psalm 16, showing how God's raising of
Jesus was indeed *in accordance with the Scriptures* (1 Corinthians
15:4). To quote Peter more fully:-

For David says concerning Him . . .'Thou wilt not abandon my soul to Hades, nor let Thy Holy One see corruption . . .' David . . . foresaw and spoke of the resurrection of the Christ, that He was not abandoned to Hades, nor did His flesh see corruption (Acts 2:25 ff.).

Christ in all the Scriptures

The subject of 'Christ in all the Scriptures' is an enthralling one. The inspired Word in the Old Testament testifies to the incarnate Word many, many times, including His resurrection from the dead:-

What of the 'Feast of the First Fruits' *on the morrow after the Sabbath* (Leviticus 23:11). Note the day. Written by Moses about 1750 BC., it yet ties in with 1 Corinthians 15:20 in a way inexplicable apart from the divine inspiration of the Scriptures. 1 Corinthians 15:20 reads: *But in fact Christ has been raised from the dead, the first fruits of those who have fallen asleep.*

What of the life of the Old Testament prophet Jonah? Jesus said of him: *For as Jonah was three days and three nights in the belly of the whale, so will the Son of Man be three days and three nights in the heart of the earth* (Matthew 12:40).

What of Hosea 5:2? *After two days He will revive us; on the third day He will raise us up.*

The Scriptures then became a new Book to Peter and John. Christ Himself said of the Old Testament Scriptures: *it is they that bear witness to Me* (John 5:39). The disciples were initially somewhat hazy in their understanding of Christ's resurrection when He first spoke about it, and equally hazy as regards the Scriptures bearing witness to Him. After Christ was raised from the dead though everything fell into place. The Scriptures began to make sense. *When therefore He was raised from the dead, His disciples . . . believed the Scripture and the word which Jesus had spoken* (John 2:22).

The resurrection of Christ enabled the disciples to understand the Scriptures. Today though, it is the opposite. We need the Scriptures and the help of the Spirit Who wrote the Scriptures to understand Christ's resurrection - its reality and its results, and to convince us that it really did occur and that it has the most revolutionary implications for our life and eternal destiny.

Chapter Six

John's Account of the First Easter Sunday

PART II :
THE RISEN CHRIST APPEARS
TO MARY MAGDALENE

But Mary stood weeping outside the tomb, and as she wept she stooped to look into the tomb; and she saw two angels in white, sitting where the body of Jesus had lain, one at the head and one at the feet. They said to her, 'Woman, why are you weeping?' She said to them, 'Because they have taken away my Lord, and I do not know where they have laid Him.' Saying this, she turned round and saw Jesus standing, but she did not know that it was Jesus. Jesus said to her, 'Woman, why are you weeping? Whom do you seek?' Supposing Him to be the gardener, she said to Him, 'Sir, if you have carried Him away, tell me where you have laid Him, and I will take Him away.' Jesus said to her, 'Mary.' She turned and said to Him in Hebrew, 'Rabboni!' (which means Teacher). Jesus said to her, 'Do not hold Me, for I have not yet ascended to the Father; but go to My brethren and say to them, I am ascending to My Father and your Father, to My God and your God.' Mary Magdalene went and said to the disciples, 'I have seen the Lord'; and she told them that He had said these things to her (John 20:11-18).

Mary Magdalene's Easter morning encounter with the risen Christ is surely one of the most tender and touching incidents of the whole Bible. Before Christ had changed Mary's life a few years earlier, it is more than likely that Mary was a person of some ill repute. Magdala was a sea port of notorious reputation. Mary's exaltation now however could not be higher. Truth is stranger than fiction, for biblical history records that it was to this very lady that the risen Christ chose to appear first. *Now when He rose early on the first day of the week, He appeared first to Mary Magdalene . . .* (Mark 16:9). Mark's concise statement here is described in more detail by John. Looking at John's details, we note that the incident begins on a sad note with:-

1. Weeping

Mary stood weeping outside the tomb . . . (v.11).

We do not like to talk about tears. Tears are the eloquent, unpretentious language of the soul. Mary was experiencing the severest disappointment she had ever faced - the loss of the best, kindest and most understanding Friend she had ever known. Her action and reaction here were totally natural ones.

During a time of sadness, the Psalmist asked God *put thou my tears in a bottle* (Psalm 56:8). None of us can expect a tear free existence this side of eternity. It is a fallen world, and tears and human misery are a consequence of this. It is good to know though that in Jesus we have a Saviour Who understands, for *Jesus wept* (John 11:35). If we belong to Jesus, we also have the sure prospect that one day we will never cry again, for the Bible says that on that Day *God will wipe away every tear from their eyes* (Revelation 7:17). The incident which we are considering now is one in which Mary's tears were dried by the risen Christ. As such, it is a mirror of the coming glory itself, when *God Himself will be with them; He will wipe away every tear from their eyes, and death shall be no more, neither shall there be mourning nor crying nor pain any more, for the former things have passed away* (Revelation 21:3,4).

Here then, is Mary in mourning. John records next that she looked through her tears, for *as she wept she stooped to look into the tomb* (v.11).

2. Seeing

Stooping to look into the tomb where she thought Jesus's embalmed body should have laid, Mary saw the most unusual sight:- *she saw two angels in white, sitting where the body of Jesus had lain, one at the head and one at the feet* (v.12).

What a sight! And what a contrast there is between this and Jesus's crucifixion three days previously. When Jesus was crucified, He was crucified between two criminals - *they crucified Him, and with Him two others, one on either side, and Jesus between them* (John 19:18). At Jesus's burial and resurrection now though, only two sinless angels were considered worthy to be there guarding Him: *two angels in white . . . one at the head and one at His feet.*

The Mercy Seat

The two angels guarding the body of Jesus remind us of two angelic beings from much earlier times, namely, the two 'cherubim' which overshadowed the mercy seat on the ark of the covenant, in the holy of holies, in the ancient tabernacle. Exodus 25:18 ff. gives the details: *And you shall make two cherubim of gold; . . . on the two ends of the mercy seat . . . Make one cherub on the one end and one cherub on the other end . . . The cherubim shall spread out their wings above, over shadowing the mercy seat with their wings.*

On the mercy seat was sprinkled the blood of atonement - that blood which made peace between a holy God and a sinful humanity. The sprinkled blood on the mercy seat was therefore vital. It was central to the Old Testament economy. What then of the two angels guarding the blessed body of Christ? It is as though John is telling us that Jesus is the true mercy seat. Jesus is the reality behind the Old Testament shadows, pictures and prefigurations, for He alone brings peace between God and humankind. Romans 3:25 tells that He is the One Whom *God put forward as a propitiation by His blood, to be received by faith.* Colossians 1:20 proclaims Him as the One *Making peace by the blood of His Christ.* It is in Jesus alone that we have the forgiveness of sins, deliverance from the wrath of God and peace with God for time and eternity. How privileged were those guardian angels guarding the true mercy seat. But how eternally blessed are we if we have been recipients of God's mercy in Christ, and have known the effectual application of His atoning blood to our sinful hearts.

Continuing with the narrative, we see that the angels asked Mary a question: *'Woman, why are you weeping?'* (v.13). The angels, of course, knew what Mary did not know, hence they knew that Mary actually had no reason to weep. Mary though still had no thoughts of a risen Saviour. Her thoughts were still as to where His earthly remains might be: *'They have taken away my Lord, and I do not know where they have laid Him'* (v.13). It is now that the narrative moves up a gear or two:-

3. Turning

Saying this she turned round and saw JESUS standing, but she did not know that it was Jesus (v.14).

Can you see a picture of Christian conversion here? Mary turned around. She turned from the grave to Jesus. She turned from the place of the dead to the Giver of eternal life. She turned from looking at the darkness to looking at the Light of the world. She turned from the sepulchre to the living Saviour!

Conversion certainly involves a turning. Paul's missionary mandate from the risen Christ was that people *may turn from darkness to light and from the power of Satan to God, that they may receive forgiveness of sins and a place among those sanctified by faith in Me* (Acts 26:18).

Mary turned to Jesus, but *she did not know that it was Jesus.* The climax of the story was yet to occur.

4. Realising

Jesus said to her, 'Woman, why are you weeping? Whom do you seek? Supposing Him to be the gardener, she said to Him, 'Sir, if

*You have carried Him away, tell me where You have laid Him . . .'
Jesus said to her 'Mary'. She turned and said to Him in Hebrew
'Rabboni!' (which means teacher)* (vv. 15,16).

Here then we have Mary's 'moment of truth' - the moment
when she realised that Jesus was alive. We know that John's
moment of truth came when he saw Jesus's undisturbed grave
clothes (20:8). It was then that *he saw and believed* (20:8). Thomas's
moment of truth was to come when the risen Christ showed
him the marks of Calvary - His wounded hands and pierced
side. It led Thomas to confess *'My Lord and my God'* (20:23).
Mary's moment though was right now. Jesus spoke her name
and she recognised His voice. It was the voice of the risen
Saviour.*'Mary.' 'Rabboni!'*

It was when Jesus spoke Mary's name that her supreme
moment of realisation came, and her tears were instantly dried.
Our names are personal to us, and bound up inextricably with
who we are. We cannot think of ourselves apart from our names.
True Christianity is intensely personal - at its very least it involves
a personal faith and an intimate relationship with the Son of
God. He is the Good Shepherd. We know Him and we hear and
heed His voice. He also knows us personally too - by name. *The
sheep hear His voice, and He calls His Own sheep by* name *and leads
them out* (John 10:3). The friendship and relationship is reciprocal.
In the New Covenant, sealed with Christ's blood, God promises
I will be their God, and they shall be My people (Jeremiah 31:33).

Just as Mary enjoyed a personal friendship with her own,
personal, living Saviour, so does every Christian. The evidence
for Christ's resurrection is objective, for sure. It is all there in the
Bible. Yet the evidence for Christ's resurrection is subjective too.
We know the living Saviour. We sing:-

He lives! He lives! Christ Jesus lives today
He walks with me, He talks with me, along life's narrow way
He lives! He lives! salvation to impart
You ask me how I know He lives?
He lives within my heart.

Mary's joy knew no bounds. She clung to the Saviour for all she was worth. It was an understandable action for her to undertake, but it led Jesus to explain something:-

5. Explaining

'Do not hold Me, for I have not yet ascended to My Father; but go to My brethren and say to them, I am ascending to My Father and your Father, to My God and your God ' (v.17).

These are intriguing words. Let us unpack them a little:-

i. *'Do not hold Me* . . . Archbishop William Temple makes the comment that Mary, and by implication all of us, 'must learn to love and trust and serve, even though she can no longer caress His feet or hear His voice pronounce her name. Not to the Lord as He tabernacled in the flesh, subject to the limitations of the body, is she to cling; but to the Lord in His perfect union with the Father. '

It was natural that Mary wanted to cling to Jesus physically, but Jesus pointed to the time when His followers everywhere would know His spiritual presence with them in a way which would be just as real. *'I in them'* (John 17:3). *For we walk by faith, not by sight* (2 Corinthians 5:7). *Christ in you* (Colossians 1:27).

ii. *'Go to My brethren* . . . Addressing the disciples as 'brethren', i.e. as those accepted in the same family, is remarkable. It reveals volumes of the Lord's grace to sinners. Mark 14:30 tells us that when Jesus was arrested *they all forsook Him and fled.* When it came to the crunch, His disciples were unreliable in their friendship towards Him. It would be understandable if Jesus had said 'Go to those cowardly deserters,' or 'Go to those unbelieving failures.' 'Go to those . . .' but He said *'Go to My brethren'.* For *He is not ashamed to call them brethren* (Hebrews 2:11). Christ's grace here - His continuing love to the undeserving and ill deserving - gives hope to us all.

iii. *'Go to My brethren and tell them, I am ascending to My Father* . . . The *Shorter Catechism* distinguishes Christ's two states

- His state of humiliation and His state of exaltation. His ascension to heaven fits into the latter category:-

> Christ's exaltation consisteth in His rising again from the dead on the third day, in ascending up into heaven, in sitting at the right hand of God the Father, and in coming to judge the world at the last day.

iv. *'I am ascending to My Father and your Father, to My God and your God.'* Noticing carefully the precise distinction that Jesus makes here between His relationship to the Father and our relationship to the Father delivers us from the Christological heresy which has plagued the world right up to the present moment:*'My Father and your Father, My God and your God.'*

Jesus is the unique Son of God. He is God's one and only Son. He is the only begotten Son of God - the eternal Son of God 'begotten, not made, being of one substance with the Father.' As such, He stands in a unique relationship to the Father. The Christian, of course, is privileged to be able to call God 'Father', but not intrinsically so, like the Lord Jesus. We can only know God as our Father by His gracious adoption - by our new birth. Jesus is the unique Son of God, and yet salvation involves becoming sons of God - sons because of our saving relationship with *the* Son. 'The Son of God became the Son of Man that the sons of men might become the sons of God.' Scripture has much to say about divine adoption: *To all who received Him (the Lord Jesus), who believed in His name, He gave power to become children of God* (John 1:12). *We were by nature children of wrath like the rest of mankind* (Ephesians 2:3). *See what love the Father has given us, that we should be called children of God; and so we are* (1 John 3:1) *God sent forth His Son . . . that we might receive adoption as sons* (Galatians 4:5).

And so the risen Christ sent Mary on her way rejoicing. He gave her some happy marching orders. Needless to say, Mary obeyed without questioning. This leads us to our final point:-

6. Telling

Mary Magdalene went and said to the disciples, 'I have seen the Lord ' . . .(v.18).

Christians are commanded to testify to the risen Saviour with both our lives and our lips. We are saved so that we may glorify God - *to declare the wonderful deeds of Him Who called you out of darkness into His marvellous light* (1 Peter 2:9). Here, we see that Mary had no difficulty in testifying to the risen Saviour. She had no reluctance in her obedience, and no lack of fluency in her speech. She *went and said to the disciples, 'I have seen the Lord.'*

Without disparaging formal training in personal witness and evangelism, surely true Christian testimony is a spontaneous overflow of an encounter with the risen Christ? It certainly was with Mary here. The Christian talks about the Saviour because *We cannot but speak of what we have seen and heard* (Acts 4:20). We rejoice in the Lord and long to share this joy with others. We benefit from the comfort of the Lord, and long to share this comfort with others. We have been saved by the risen Lord, and we long to share this greatest of blessings with anyone and everyone. People have always had their objections and arguments against both the Christian Faith and Christian people. But you cannot really argue with personal experience: *'I have seen the Lord.'* A transforming encounter with the risen Christ will surely give us all the conviction and eloquence we need.

And so we leave this lovely account of Mary's meeting with the risen Christ in Joseph's garden, on that first Easter morning. Perhaps the hymn writer had this incident in mind when he wrote the following lines:-

I come to the garden alone
While the dew is still on the roses
And the voice I hear
Falling on my ear
The Son of God discloses

And He walks with me, and He talks with me
And He tells me I am His Own
And the joy we share
As we tarry there
None other has ever known

He speaks, and the sound of His voice
Is so sweet the birds hush their singing
And the melody
That He gave to me
Within my heart is ringing

I'd stay in the garden with Him
Though the night around me be falling
But He bids me go
Through the voice of woe
His voice to me is calling

And He walks with me, and He talks with me
And He tells me I am His Own
And the joy we share
As we tarry there
None other has ever known.

Chapter Seven

Behind Closed Doors

On the evening of that day, the first day of the week, the doors being shut where the disciples were, for fear of the Jews, Jesus came and stood among them and said to them, 'Peace be with you.' When He had said this, He showed them His hands and His side. Then the disciples were glad when they saw the Lord. Jesus said to them again, 'Peace be with you. As the Father has sent Me, even so I send you.' And when He had said this, He breathed on them, and said to them, 'Receive the Holy Spirit. If you forgive the sins of any, they are forgiven; if you retain the sins of any, they are retained.'

Now Thomas, one of the twelve, called the Twin, was not with them when Jesus came. So the other disciples told him, 'We have seen the Lord.' But he said to them, 'Unless I see in His hands the print of the nails, and place my finger in the mark of the nails, and place my hand in His side, I will not believe.'

Eight days later, His disciples were again in the house, and Thomas was with them. The doors were shut, but Jesus came and stood among them, and said, 'Peace be with you.' Then He said to Thomas, 'Put your finger here, and see my hands; and put out your hand, and place it in My side; do not be faithless, but believing.' Thomas answered Him, 'My Lord and My God!' Jesus said to Him, 'Have you believed because you have seen Me? Blessed are those who have not seen and yet believe.'

Now Jesus did many other signs in the presence of the disciples, which are not written in this book; but these are written that you may believe that Jesus is the Christ, the Son of God, and that believing you may have life in His name (John 20:19-31).

John 20:19-31 takes us back to the evening of the very first Easter Sunday and the first Sunday after that first Easter Sunday. In these sacred verses, the Holy Spirit has allowed us to see the risen Saviour appearing to His frightened disciples, who were initially cowering away, behind closed doors.

We are dealing here with history and not mythology, reality and not fantasy. *To them (i.e. the disciples) He presented Himself alive after His passion by many proofs, appearing to them during forty days, and speaking of the kingdom of God* (Acts 1:4). We have seen that the evidence for Christ's resurrection rests mainly on i. the fact that His tomb was empty and ii. the fact that the risen Christ appeared. Here now we are dealing with two of the resurrection appearances of Christ:-

> In the upper chamber
> Where the ten in fear
> Gathered, sad and troubled
> Jesus did appear
> So, O Lord, this evening
> Bid our sorrows cease
> Breathing on us Saviour
> Say 'I give you peace.'

There is always a danger of missing the obvious - of not seeing the wood for the trees. This being so, we note first of all:-

1. The Divine Presence

On the evening of that day, the first day of the week, the doors being shut where the disciples were, for fear of the Jews, JESUS CAME AND STOOD AMONG THEM . . . He showed them His hands and His side . . . (v.19 ff.).

Here we have the divine presence - the presence of the risen Christ, before the disciples' very eyes. All ten of them certainly could not have been hallucinating at the same time. The disciples were at this point a sorry group, cast down and down cast until, when they least expected it, JESUS CAME AND STOOD AMONG THEM.

We state again that the Christian Faith is a resurrection Faith. It preaches and proclaims that the Saviour Who died on Good Friday rose from the grave on Easter Sunday. The Christian Faith is also a resurrection Faith because it testifies that the risen Saviour gives new life to all who believe in Him: He raises us up from spiritual death. *And you He made alive, when you were dead through the trespasses and sins in which you once walked* (Ephesians 2:1). 'Resurrection' is one of the key words of the Christian Faith. As the earliest Christian creed states:-

I delivered to you as of first importance what I also received, that Christ died for our sins in accordance with the Scriptures, that He was buried, that He was raised on the third day in accordance with the Scriptures (1 Corinthians 15:3,4).

Christ's resurrection is the final proof that He is none less than the Son of God and God the Son - *designated Son of God in power according to the Spirit of holiness by His resurrection from the dead, Jesus Christ our Lord* (Romans 1:4).

Christ's resurrection is His ultimate vindication, evidence of His power to save, and seal of God the Father's approval on His atoning work on the cross. He *was put to death for our trespasses and raised for our justification* (Romans 4:25).

The ten frightened disciples had met the risen Christ. *Jesus came and stood among them.* There was no doubt at all that this was the same Jesus Who had been crucified. He identified Himself so: *He showed them His hands and His side.* John's account then says in verse 20: *Then the disciples were glad when they saw the Lord.* Every effect has a cause. What then explains the change that came about in the disciples? They were now characterised by gladness and not gloom, faith and not fear. The only explanation is that Christ had risen. *Jesus came and stood among them . . . Then the disciples were glad when they saw the Lord.* An encounter with the risen Saviour always results in gladness:-

Who can cheer the heart like Jesus?
By His presence all Divine?
True and tender, pure and precious
O how blest to call Him mine!

All that thrills my soul is Jesus
He is more than life to me
And the fairest of ten thousand
In my blessed Lord I see.

2. The Divine Peace

Jesus came and stood among them and said 'Peace be with you'
(v.19). *Jesus said to them again 'Peace be with you . . .'* (v.21).
Here we have the divine peace. It was the common Hebrew greeting, 'Shalom', and yet, coming from the lips of Jesus, it was much more than this. Gripped with fear as the disciples were, this divine 'Shalom' was more than welcome. *'Peace be with you.'* 'Although this was the ordinary salutation, it means more here, for the words conveyed the Master's Own gift of peace.'

Isaiah 9:6 describes Jesus as *the Prince of Peace*. It is Jesus alone Who can give us peace with God, and it is Jesus alone Who can impart the peace of God to the human soul. In His Own words:- *'Peace I leave with you; My peace I give to you; not as the world gives do I give to you. Let not your hearts be troubled, neither let them be afraid.'*

Back to the Cross

Notice now a very significant detail as the risen Christ imparted His peace to the disciples. *Jesus came and stood among them and said to them 'Peace be with you.' When He had said this He showed them His hands and His side*. ... that is, He showed them the marks of His crucifixion - the marks of Calvary. All this is highly significant. It tells us graphically that our peace is based on His pains; our salvation is based on His sacrifice; our eternal well being rests on His excruciating wounds. *He was wounded for our transgressions, He was bruised for our iniquities; upon Him was the chastisement that made us whole, and with His stripes we are healed* (Isaiah 53:5). *Jesus . . . said to them 'Peace be with you.' When He had said this He showed them His hands and His side.* Christ showed them the physical evidence that salvation had been wrought. He showed them why the believing sinner may have peace with God - because Jesus died for the sinner on Calvary's cross. Jesus alone can bestow the forgiveness of sins and peace with God. This is the Christian Gospel in a nutshell: Peace with God through the death of Christ. The Scriptures are crystal clear on this point:-

Therefore, since we are justified by faith we have peace with God through our Lord Jesus Christ (Romans 5:1).

But now in Christ Jesus you who once were far off have been brought near in the blood of Christ. For He is our peace . . . (Ephesians 2:13,14).

. . . making peace by the blood of His cross (Colossians 1:20).

It is by the redeeming work of Jesus that we receive the greatest blessing of all, namely, peace with God - the forgiveness of sins, reconciliation to God and fellowship with Him for time and eternity.

3. The Divine Power

Jesus said to them again, 'Peace be with you. As the Father has sent Me, even so I send you.' (v.21).

The Christian Faith is a missionary Faith - one of its features is that of 'sending.' As Christ Himself was sent by the Father to procure salvation (c.f. Galatians 4:4 ff.), so now Christ sends out His disciples to proclaim salvation. Notice though that Christ did not - and still does not - send His disciples out unaided. With the sending comes the empowering: *And when He had said this, He breathed on them, and said to them, 'Receive the Holy Spirit'* (v.22). Here is the divine power - a kind of anticipation of the coming of the Holy Spirit in power at Pentecost, fifty days later. Christ thus commissioned them, and Christ also enabled them to carry out His commission - He granted them the help of His Holy Spirit.

Apart from the help of the Holy Spirit - that is God Himself working in and through His human vessels - all Christian ministry is in vain. Just as Adam was mere lifeless clay until God breathed the breath of life into him, likewise no one will ever be born again unless the Lord Jesus, as it were, breathes new life into them by His Holy Spirit. The Holy Spirit is essential if there is to be any authentic Christian salvation or any fruitful Christian service. We need the living, life-giving Holy Spirit of God.

But what did the Holy Spirit equip the disciples to do? The answer is 'Preach the Gospel.' *'Receive the Holy Spirit. If you forgive the sins of any, they are forgiven, if you retain the sins of any they are retained'* (v.23).

This verse needs careful interpretation. We know from the Bible that the Gospel is all about the forgiveness of sins, and we know from the Bible that only God Himself can forgive sins - *'Who can forgive sins but God alone?'*

> Although it is not in the power of man to forgive sins, man can pronounce forgiveness on the basis of what God has done in Christ. This is through the agency of the Holy Spirit within him, making him Christ's ambassador. Those who refuse to accept forgiveness (i.e. those who refuse Christ) inevitably retain their sins.

The verse therefore is not as obscure as some have made out it to be. It refers to the preaching of the Gospel - the Gospel which the disciples had been empowered to preach:-

> Those who proclaim the Gospel are in effect forgiving or not forgiving

sins, depending on whether the hearers accept or reject the Lord Jesus Christ.

All that the Christian can do is announce the message of forgiveness. God (alone) performs the miracle of forgiveness. If sinners will believe on Jesus Christ, we can authoritatively declare to them that their sins have been forgiven; but we are not the ones who provide forgiveness.

I am writing to you little children because your sins are forgiven for His sake (1 John 2:12).

Moving on in John's account, we come now to its climactic moment. We can consider this under the heading of:-

4. The Divine Praise

John's account of the risen Christ's appearance in the upper room contains a spontaneous exclamation and proclamation of divine praise - praise uttered by Thomas in verse twenty eight: *Thomas answered Him, 'My Lord and my God.'* We come now to the testimony of 'doubting Thomas' - a testimony which occurred one week after the events we have considered so far.

How did Thomas's expression of praise come about? John tells us. He says *Now Thomas, one of the twelve, called the Twin, was not with them when Jesus came.* We are not given the reasons for Thomas's absence. He no doubt had his own reasons or excuses. The lesson for us though is that it does not pay to be absent from the gathering of the Lord's people. If we stay away, we may miss out on the special presence of the Saviour, as Thomas did. Thomas, being absent the first time, missed out on the blessing and reassuring words of peace that the others were privileged to receive. He was not there. *So the other disciples told*

*him 'We have seen the Lord.' But he (Thomas) said to them, 'Unless I
see in His hands the print of the nails, and place my finger in the mark
of the nails, and place my hand in His side, I will not believe'* (v.28).

We have already seen how the Bible paints people 'warts
and all.' No attempt is made to sweep Thomas's doubts and
scepticism under the carpet. He was adamant that he would
only believe if the evidence was there in front of him. But what
happened? Well the Lord gave him the irrefutable evidence
which he sought:-

*Eight days later, His disciples were again in the house, and
Thomas was with them. The doors were shut, but Jesus came and stood
among them, and said, 'Peace be with you.' Then He said to Thomas,
'Put your finger here, and see My hands; and put out your hand and
place it in My side; do not be faithless, but believing'* (v.26 ff.).

No one had told the Lord about Thomas's doubts - yet He
knew them. Omniscience is an attribute of deity. The Lord quoted
back to Thomas his very own words. Thomas now needed no
more proof. His reaction now was not that of a sceptical, scientific
enquirer, but that of a reverent worshipper. *Thomas answered Him
'MY LORD AND MY GOD.'*

'MY LORD AND MY GOD.' It is here that John's Gospel
reaches its climax. On seeing the crucified, risen Saviour, Thomas
was led to confess his faith in the absolute, total and irrefutable
deity of the Lord Jesus Christ. *My Lord and my God.* The Bible
teaches that there is but one God, and to worship any one or
anything other than the one true God is gross idolatry. Here
though we see Thomas worshipping Jesus. He confessed to Him
'My Lord and my God.' Jesus accepted his confession. He did not
rebuke Thomas for idolatry. It is further evidence of Christ's
deity. Christianity is Christ and Jesus Christ is God. He is the
Son of God and God the Son, co-equal with God the Father and
God the Holy Spirit in the unity of the mystery of the blessed
Trinity. *'My Lord and my God.'* John's Gospel cannot go any higher
than this. The deity of Christ is one of the fundamentals of the
Christian Faith. If we open John's Gospel anywhere, we will see
Christ's deity somewhere. His walk, works, words and worth
proclaim that here we are dealing with God in the flesh. *For in*

Him the whole fulness of deity dwells bodily (Colossians 2:9) -'*My
Lord and my God.*'

> Thou art the everlasting Word
> The Father's only Son
> God manifestly seen and heard
> And heaven's beloved One
>
> In thee most perfectly expressed
> The Father's glories shine
> Of the full Deity possessed
> Eternally Divine
>
> Worthy, O Lamb of God art Thou
> That every knee to Thee should bow.

At this point though, someone may raise an objection. Is
it not the case that Thomas had an unfair advantage over us?
Not necessarily, as we shall see when we consider what the Lord
Jesus said next.

5. The Divine Pronouncement

*Jesus said to him, 'Have you believed because you have seen
Me? Blessed are those who have not seen and yet believe'* (v.29).

In this divine pronouncement we actually have a beatitude
- '*Blessed are those who have not seen and yet believe.*'

Thomas was certainly privileged - as were the other
disciples. Yet, truth be told, they had no great advantage over
us. The Lord is referring here to future believers, and He says
here that it is not necessary to see Him with our physical eyes in
order to believe. Thomas, and the other disciples saw Him. Yet
they were saved, not by seeing Jesus, but by believing in Jesus -
just as we are today. If we believe in Jesus, our blessedness is
equal to theirs. '*Blessed are those who have not seen and yet believe.*'
1 Peter 1:8,9 is the Bible's own commentary which further
explains these words of the Lord:-

Without having seen Him you love Him; though you do not now see Him you believe in Him and rejoice with unutterable and exalted joy. As the outcome of your faith you obtain the salvation of your souls.

'Blessed are those who have not seen and yet believe.'

This statement of Jesus is for those whose faith rests on the report of others. Such faith is of a nobler order than Thomas's. It is the kind of faith which has sustained the Christian church to the present time. Ultimately, true faith must always be independent of sight.

'Blessed are those who have not seen and yet believe.'

Jesus, these eyes have never seen
That radiant form of Thine
The veil of sense hangs dark between
Thy blessed face and mine

Yet though I have not seen and still
Must rest in faith alone
I love Thee dearest Lord, and will
Unseen, but not unknown.

Finally, in verse thirty one, John reveals to us his purpose in telling us, not just about Thomas and about the crucified and risen Christ, but in writing the twenty one chapters of his whole Gospel. This takes us to:-

6. The Divine Purpose

John had no hidden agenda. He was honest and completely above board. He wrote his Gospel to be a kind of Christian manifesto. Note the divine purpose of his Gospel:-

These are written that you may believe that Jesus is the Christ, the Son of God, and that believing you may have life in His name (v.31).

Although this verse is near the end of John's book, it actually is the clue verse and the key verse to all that John wrote. Unpacking it, we see:-

i. John's purpose in writing his Gospel was that you may believe that Jesus is the *Christ* - that is, the Messiah, the anointed One, the one sent by God to redeem His people. Jesus is the *Christ* - our prophet, priest and king.

ii. John's purpose in writing his Gospel was that you may believe that Jesus is *the Son of God.* Thomas, we saw, confessed to Jesus *'My Lord and my God.'* John would have all his readers do the same, and so he recorded a selection of Jesus's signs and sayings, works and words which give the clearest evidence that He is indeed the Son of God and God the Son. John's purpose in writing is to bring you to such a clear cut confession as Thomas.

iii. John's purpose in writing his Gospel was that you may *believe* - that is, that you may put your faith in Jesus, and receive Him as your own, personal Saviour. *To all who received Him, who believed in His name, He gave power to become children of God* (John 1:12). The *Shorter Catechism* states:- 'Faith in Jesus Christ is a saving grace, whereby we receive and rest upon Him alone for salvation, as He is offered to us in the Gospel.'

iv. John's purpose in writing his Gospel was that *you may have life in His name.* Here we are dealing with 'eternal life' - the eternal life which ensues from believing in Jesus; the eternal life which results from having a saving relationship with Him. Only Jesus can give eternal life, and only faith can receive this greatest of all gifts. *The free gift of God is eternal life in Christ Jesus our Lord* (Romans 6:23). Eternal life means experiencing the very life of God in our souls today. Eternal life is a divine quality of life - heaven on earth today. Eternal life is knowing Jesus: *This is eternal life that they know Thee the only true God and Jesus Christ Whom Thou hast sent.* Eternal life is enjoying the salvation of Christ - the forgiveness of sins, peace with God and fellowship with Him both here and hereafter.

This then was the reason why John wrote his Gospel, and God preserved his Gospel: that we might have eternal life - life through the crucified and risen Saviour, the Saviour Who is the Son of God.

Chapter Eight

The Saviour on the Shore -
'It is the Lord!'

After this Jesus revealed Himself again to the disciples by the Sea of Tiberias; and He revealed Himself in this way. Simon Peter, Thomas called the Twin, Nathaniel of Cana in Galilee, the sons of Zebedee, and two others of His disciples were together. Simon Peter said to them, 'I am going fishing.' They said to him, 'We will go with you.' They went out and got into the boat; but that night they caught nothing.

Just as day was breaking, Jesus stood on the beach; yet the disciples did not know that it was Jesus. Jesus said to them, 'Children, have you any fish?' They answered Him, 'No.' He said to them, 'Cast the net on the right side of the boat, and you will find some.' So they cast it, and now they were not able to haul it in, for the quantity of fish. That disciple whom Jesus loved said to Peter, 'It is the Lord!' When Simon Peter heard that it was the Lord, he put on his clothes, for he was stripped for work, and sprang into the sea. But the other disciples came in the boat, dragging the net full of fish, for they were not far from the land, but about a hundred yards off.

When they got out on the land, they saw a charcoal fire there, with fish lying on it, and bread. Jesus said to them, 'Bring some of the fish that you have just caught.' So Simon Peter went aboard and hauled the net ashore, full of large fish, a hundred and fifty-three of them; and although there were so many, the net was not torn. Jesus said to them, 'Come and have breakfast.' Now none of the disciples dared ask Him, 'Who are you?' They knew it was the Lord. Jesus came and took the bread and gave it to them, and so with the fish. This was now the third time that Jesus was revealed to the disciples after He was raised from the dead.

When they had finished breakfast, Jesus said to Simon Peter, 'Simon, son of John, do you love Me more than these?' He said to Him, 'Yes, Lord; You know that I love You.' He said to him, 'Feed My lambs.' A second time He said to him, 'Simon, son of John, do you love Me?' He said to him, 'Yes, Lord; You know that I love You.' He said to him, 'Tend My sheep.' He said to him the third time, 'Simon, son of John, do you love Me?' Peter was grieved because He said to him the third time, 'Do you love Me?' And he said to Him, 'Lord, You know everything; You know that I love you.' Jesus said to him, 'Feed My sheep. Truly, truly, I say to you, when you were young, you girded yourself and walked where you would; but when you are old, you will stretch out your hands, and another will gird you and carry you where you do not wish to go.' (This He said to show by what death he was to glorify God.) And after this He said to him, 'Follow Me.'

Peter turned and saw following them the disciple whom Jesus loved, who had lain close to His breast at the supper and had said, 'Lord, who is it that is going to betray you?' When Peter saw him, he said to Jesus, 'Lord, what about this man?' Jesus said to him, 'If it is My will that he remain until I come, what is that to you? Follow Me!' The saying spread abroad among the brethren that this disciple was not to die; yet Jesus did not say to him that he was not to die, but, 'If it is My will that he remain until I come, what is that to you?'

This is the disciple who is bearing witness to these things, and who has written these things; and we know that his testimony is true.

But there are also many other things which Jesus did; were every one of them to be written, I suppose that the world itself could not contain the books that would be written (John 21).

Introduction

In John 21 we are confronted with *the third time that Jesus was revealed to the disciples after He was raised from the dead* (v.14). In Mark 14:28 Jesus prophesied *'But after I am raised up, I will go before you to Galilee'*. And His prophecy came true. He most surely was raised up, and He most surely went before the disciples to Galilee. The evidence for this is in this twenty first chapter of John which we are considering now.

We turn then to the third resurrection appearance of the Lord Jesus to His disciples, and the fourth resurrection appearance of the Lord Jesus as described by John in all. At this time the disciples were out fishing on the Sea of Galilee when they again met up with the risen Christ:-

> *Jesus stood on the beach* (v.4).
> *That disciple whom Jesus loved said . . . 'It is the Lord!'* (v.7).
> *They knew it was the Lord* (v.12).

John 21 is the very last chapter of John's incomparable book, and in it we come face to face again with the Christ Who conquered the grave. This last chapter of John's therefore is in line with all of John's chapters - *written that you may believe that Jesus is the Christ, the Son of God, and that believing you may have life in His name* (John 20:31). Selecting some of the salient points we note:-

1. Fishing

At least seven of Jesus's disciples were fishermen by occupation. *Simon Peter said to them 'I am going fishing.' They said to him, 'We will go with you'* (v.3). Opinions are divided as to whether Peter and his friends should have gone fishing at this time. Some believe that Peter was backsliding somewhat here, as he had been given a full-time calling to leave fishing for fish, for a life dedicated to fishing for the souls of men. Others though consider that it was legitimate for Peter to employ the skills he had as a way of paying the bills.

It is interesting to note that the New Testament uses fishing to picture evangelism. Jesus told a parable in Matthew 13:47 ff. which ran:-

'The kingdom of heaven is like a net which was thrown into the sea and gathered fish of every kind; when it was full men drew it ashore and sat down and sorted the good into vessels but threw away the bad. So will it be at the close of the age . . .

It was most fitting therefore that many of Jesus's disciples were originally fishermen. Both fishing and evangelism need courage, dedication, the ability to take orders, the ability to work as a team, and the ability to 'keep on keeping on' inspite of difficulties and rough waters.

Fishing and evangelism are similar, and yet they have a contrast. In fishing, living fish are caught and then they die. In evangelism though, dead souls are caught and given eternal life. *And you He made alive, when you were dead through the trespasses and sins in which you once walked . . .* (Ephesians 2:1).

The disciples had 'gone fishing.' But all was not well. *They went out and got into the boat; but that night they caught nothing* (v.5). *'Children, have you any fish?' They answered . . . 'No'* (v.5). They worked hard, and they toiled all night . . . but it was all in vain. They caught nothing. What a graphic illustration of Jesus's words in John 15:5 we have here: *'For apart from Me, you can do nothing.'* And what an illustration, we fear, of much church activity today - busy, but fruitless. Any activity not of the Lord - *'I* am going fishing' - is sure to be fruitless, for it lacks the Lord's blessing and direction. Apart from Jesus's blessing, all of our efforts are in vain. But notice the difference the blessing of Jesus makes:-

'Cast the net on the right side of the boat, and you will find some.' So they cast it, and now they were not able to haul it in, for the quantity of fish (v.6). *. . . the other disciples came in the boat, dragging the net full of fish . . .*(v.8).

What a difference Jesus makes! There can only be success with Him. If evangelism is to 'catch' men with the truth of the Gospel, oh to be able to fish under the supervision, direction and blessing of the Lord Jesus Christ. Oh to fish *on the right side of the boat.*

Verse 11 tells us how *Simon Peter went aboard and hauled the net ashore, full of large fish, a hundred and fifty three of them; and though there were so many, the net was not torn.* The practice of 'counting the catch' was a standard procedure in New Testament times. They would fish with a large drag net, and *when it was full, men drew it ashore and sat down and sorted the good into vessels but threw away the bad* (Matthew 13:48). The catch here was a distinct number, one hundred and fifty three fish. The nets were heaving, but they did not break under the strain.

According to the Bible, God too has a distinct number of people - His elect, those chosen in Christ before the foundation of the world. He will most surely gather every one of these people into the Gospel net of eternal salvation. His net will not tear. His people will not escape. God's great multitude will surely enjoy His eternal salvation for ever more. *Then I looked, and lo, on Mount Zion stood the Lamb, and with Him a hundred and forty four thousand who had His name and His Father's name written on their foreheads* (Revelation 14:1).

2. Fellowshipping

Jesus said to them, 'Come and have breakfast' (v.12). Jesus came and took the bread and gave it to them, and so with the fish (v.13).

Here, the disciples were actually feasting with the risen Lord. 'God and man at table are sat down.' In Bible times, sharing a meal with someone was symbolic of friendship. You did not eat with your enemies! The disciples then enjoyed a meal with Jesus. It is simple and yet profound, but such fellowship almost encapsulates what it is to be a Christian, both now and eternally, when we sit down at the marriage supper of the Lamb:-

'The kingdom of heaven may be compared with a king who gave a marriage feast for his son (Matthew 22:2).

'Behold, I stand at the door and knock; if any one hears My voice and opens the door, I will come in to him and eat with him and he with Me (Revelation 3:20).

Blessed are those who are invited to the marriage supper of the Lamb (Revelation 19:9).

'Come and have breakfast' was such a gracious invitation. It gave the disciples opportunity to dry off, get warm, satisfy their hunger, and most of all, enjoy the friendship and fellowship of the risen Christ Himself. 'Where Jesus is, 'tis heaven there'. The disciples must have felt so at home - almost like heaven on earth. This picture of the disciples eating with the Saviour is truly marvellous, and yet, because of God's grace in Christ, it is just the same today. We too may know and enjoy fellowship with the risen Saviour, because it is still true that *This Man receives sinners and eats with them* (Luke 15:2).

> Sinners Jesus will receive
> Sound this word of grace to all
> Who the heavenly pathway leave
> All who linger, all who fall
>
> Christ receiveth sinful men
> Even me with all my sin
> Purged from every spot and stain
> Heaven with Him I'll enter in
>
> Sing it o'er and o'er again
> Christ receiveth sinful men
> Make the message loud and plain
> Christ receiveth sinful men.

3. Forgiving

In John 18 we read of Peter's denying His Master three times. It was the lowest point of Peter's life. As Bishop Ryle used to say 'The best of men are men at best.' In Acts 2 though, we read of Peter's preaching his Master, and the three thousand souls which were converted as a result of Peter's preaching. All this is within four consecutive chapters of the Bible. What accounts for the difference in Peter, between his cowardly denial of Jesus in John 18 and his fearless proclamation of Jesus in Acts 2? The answer is in the incident we are now considering. The risen Christ forgave Peter and restored him to Himself and future usefulness.

In John 18:18 we read that Peter denied his Lord while standing around *a charcoal fire, because it was cold . . . Peter was with them, standing and warming himself.* Here in John 21:9 we read similarly of *a charcoal fire there, with fish lying on it and bread.* Here we have a much 'happier' charcoal fire. The fire of failure and betrayal was now replaced by the fire of forgiveness and blessing.

Peter had denied Jesus three times. Now, as Jesus restored him to Himself, Jesus correspondingly issued a three-fold question:-

'Simon, son of John, do you love Me more than these? . . .

A second time He said to him, 'Simon, son of John, do you love Me? . . .

He said to him the third time, 'Simon, son of John, do you love Me? . . .'

Peter's three-fold denial was cancelled out! *I, even I am He Who blots out your transgressions for My Own sake, and I will not remember your sins'* (Isaiah 43:25). Praise God that failure need not be final. There is restorative grace with the Lord. Which one of us has not fallen? Which one of us can say that we will never fall? But with God there is still pardon, hope, forgiveness and restoration. Peter would tell you so. Years later he wrote *The God of all grace . . . will restore you* (1 Peter 5:10). Scripture has great encouragement for those, even of God's people, who, having failed, still seek God for mercy:-

Rejoice not over me, O my enemy; when I fall, I shall rise (Micah 7:8).

If we say we have no sin we deceive ourselves and the truth is not in us. If we confess our sins He is faithful and just, and will forgive our sins and cleanse us from all unrighteousness (1 John 1:8,9).

There was forgiveness with the risen Christ - and there is still forgiveness with the risen Christ.

Mine is an unchanging love
Higher than the heights above
Deeper than the depths beneath
Free and faithful, strong as death.

But what followed on from Peter's forgiveness and restoration? The answer is: Christian responsibility:-

4. Feeding

'Feed My lambs (v.15).
'Tend My sheep (v.16).
'Feed My sheep (v.17).

The Lord did not write Peter off, but gave him the responsibility of being a pastor - one who cares for the flock of God. Scripture often uses the metaphor of sheep to describe the people of God. *For He is our God, and we are the people of His pasture and the sheep of His hand* (Psalm 95:7).

The picture therefore has changed from that of a fisherman catching fish, to that of a shepherd caring for his flock. It was early days, but we know that Peter certainly did fulfil his calling and commission. Years later, in 1 Peter 5:5, he wrote this to his fellow pastors: *I exhort the elders among you, as a fellow elder . . . Tend the flock of God that is your charge.*

Peter was certainly no Pope. He describes himself here as *a fellow elder* - one who had equal parity. His main qualification for this role was that he knew himself to be a forgiven sinner. He knew his own heart, and he also knew the grace of the Lord Jesus for a sinner such as himself. He also knew that he loved the Lord Jesus, albeit imperfectly, albeit inspite of his past and present faults and failings.

Peter then was to be a shepherd or pastor, one who cared for God's flock. He was not a Pope but a pastor - an under-shepherd under the Lord Jesus Christ, Whom Scripture describes as the Good Shepherd, the Great Shepherd and the Chief Shepherd (John 10:11, Hebrews 13:20 and 1 Peter 5:4). And these principles are still relevant today:-

If we are believers, we are like rescued sheep. We are now in God's fold and part of His flock. As such, we need to be fed spiritually. We are to be fed by the Lord Jesus Christ Himself, Who feeds us through the faithful exposition of His Word, through the mouth and ministry of His under shepherds - those who are truly called and ordained to pastor His Church.

Today, perhaps more than any other day, we have to beware of false shepherds - the fierce wolves who attack the flock of God, either blatantly or subtly. Sheep need to be fed - yet how many churches really provide the needed sustenance for God's flock? Ezekiel 34 warns us against such 'shepherds': *Ho, shepherds of Israel who have been feeding yourselves. Should not shepherds feed the sheep? You do not feed the sheep.*

How imperative it is to be under a Pastor who is himself under *the* Pastor - under the Good Shepherd, the Lord Jesus Christ, the One Who said '*I am the Good Shepherd; I know My own and My Own know Me . . . and I lay down My life for the sheep* (John 10:14 ff.).

5. Following

'*Follow Me*' (v.19)
'*Lord, what about this man?' Jesus said to him, 'If it is My will that he remain until I come, what is that to you? Follow Me*' (v.21).

'*Follow Me*' is a command of the Lord Jesus to Peter then and to us now. The tense of the verb used here is continuous - 'Follow Me, keep on following Me, continue to follow Me.' Such a command is actually an implicit sign of deity, for only God can command our total allegiance. In 1 Kings 18:21, Elijah issued the challenge: '*If the LORD is God, follow Him; but if Baal, then follow him..*'

The picture therefore has changed yet again. We have moved from the fisherman, to the shepherd and now we have the picture of the disciple - one who follows the Lord Jesus. Peter no doubt recalled Jesus's words some three years earlier:'*Follow Me and I will make you become fishers of men*' (Mark 1:17). Mark notes that *immediately they left their nets and followed Him..*

Following Jesus sounds simple, and in one sense it is. Yet how easily do we get diverted from following Him with a single mind. How soon do we stray into by-path meadow. This even happened to Peter. Peter started to wonder about John, and the Lord's plans for him. Jesus's reply to Peter - and to us - though was *'What is that to you? Follow Me.'*

We too have to beware of looking at others. Other people, even other Christians, can have the effect of making us take our eyes off the Lord. God no doubt has His plans for them, but these may not be His plans for us. We are not called to look to others, nor our circumstances, nor even to our own feelings. We are called to follow the Lord. Comparing ourselves with others can make us either vain or bitter. Other people, on the surface, always seem to have a better ride than us! When such is our temptation, we must recall the Lord's words here: *'What is that to you? Follow Me.'* If we were privy to God's perfect plans for us, we would surely not want to be any one else, and be totally content with whatever He sends us or withholds from us. Jesus says to us personally: *'Follow Me.'* Hebrews 12:1,2 takes this further when it urges: *Let us run with perseverance the race that is set before us, LOOKING TO JESUS the pioneer and perfecter of our faith.*

'Follow Me.' *'The sheep follow Him, for they know His voice* (John 10:4). Finally, we consider:-

6. Focusing

We wonder what kind of emotions John felt as he finally completed his Gospel. How did he feel when he lifted his quill after putting down the final full-stop?

John closes his Gospel by affirming the truth - the literal 'Gospel truth' - of all that he has written. *This is the disciple who is bearing witness to these things and who has written these things; and we know that his testimony is true.*

If you have ever visited the National Library of Wales in Aberystwyth, you will know that it is very easy to get lost in that enormous building. The National Library is said to contain every book ever published in the United Kingdom. In John's final verse of his Gospel, he says that what he has written is only a selection of what Jesus did - selected for us under the superintendence of the Holy Spirit. It had to be a selection, as the world itself - let alone the National Library - could not contain all the books that could have been written about the incomparable Christ:-

But there are also many other things which Jesus did; were every one of them to be written, I suppose that the world itself could not contain the books that would be written (v.25).

This notwithstanding, John is adamant that what he has written is true. *We know that his testimony (or witness) is true.* The word 'testimony' or 'witness' is a key word in John's Gospel. He uses it some forty seven times in all. How earnest John was to let us know that his account of the Lord Jesus was a totally authentic one - fact not fiction, history not mythology, Divine truth not a human tale.

It is good that we can trust the record of the whole Bible and the Gospel record of John in particular, for apart from the Word of God, the Bible, we would know nothing of the Saviour and nothing of God's plan and way of salvation. Thank God then that His Word is true and dependable. The Word of God is as trustworthy as the God of the Word! 'True' is one of the trademarks of the Bible. God Himself has put His stern check and trademark into His Word affirming that this is so. Read these verses, the first from Moses's day, the second from the book of Proverbs, and the third from the very last book of the Book:-

You shall not add to the Word which I command you, nor take from it (Deuteronomy 4:2).

Every word of God proves true . . . Do not add to His words lest He rebuke you, and you be found a liar (Proverbs 30:6).

I warn every one who hears the words of the prophecy of this book: if any one adds to them, God will add to him the plagues described in this book, and if any one takes away from the words of the book of this prophecy, God will take away his share in the tree of life and in the holy city, which are described in this book (Revelation 22:18,19).

John's testimony to the life, death and resurrection of Jesus is therefore absolutely true. He is the Christ, the Son of God, and whoever believes in Him will not perish, but have eternal life.

Soli Deo Gloria

EPILOGUE

The Day of Resurrection!
Earth, tell it out abroad
The Passover of gladness
The Passover of God!
From death to life eternal
From earth unto the sky
Our Christ hath brought us over
With hymns of victory

Our hearts be pure from evil
That we may see aright
The Lord in rays eternal
Of resurrection-light
And listening to His accents
May hear so calm and plain
His own 'All hail,' and hearing
May raise the victor strain

Now let the heav'ns be joyful
And earth her song begin
The round world keep high triumph
And all that is therein
Let all things seen and unseen
Their notes of gladness blend
For CHRIST THE LORD IS RISEN
Our joy that hath no end.